ENDORSEMENTS FOR
YOU MATTER

You Matter beautifully demonstrates the ongoing effect a spiritual lineage can have on an individual, a family, a nation and the world. A legacy of character and commitment was poured into Bishop Zink at an early age. He is committed to a special call on his life to be a blessing and a voice of encouragement for all people.

Dr. Marilyn Hickey
President – Marilyn Hickey Ministries

There has never been a more relevant time and season where the Body of Christ needs to know and understand the value of legacy and promise. Bishop Paul Zink is a longtime friend that I have great respect for as a minister of the gospel, as well as being a strong man of valor.

Bishop Paul Zink is a powerful scholar and teacher with fresh insight that will inspire you and impact your life with the revelation of the Word that will come alive throughout this book. I encourage you to not only read this book but apply the word and put this content into practice. It will enrich your life and deepen your relationship with Christ.

Perry Stone
Founder and President of Voice of Evangelist
Host of Manna-Fest *TV Program*

Leaders from politicians to patriarchs worry a lot, or at least talk a lot about legacy. The problem is they do not do a lot. Bishop Zink charts the course for any who will listen. Anyone concerned about leaving a legacy should get this book.

Dr. Mark Rutland
Founder and President of Global Servants

I would like to highly recommend this book by Bishop Paul Zink. We at CGI have come to know this man of God over many years as a member of our honored CGI Board of Directors.

He has written a wonderful book advising believers of the great importance of our legacies, which are more valuable than gold.

A life that is well lived in all integrity, purity, and righteousness is a goal to be pursued throughout all of our lives. The greatest heritage to leave posterity is your life lived to the fullest in pursuit of the Maker, Jesus Christ.

All civilizations are created and inspired by those who have legacies of self-sacrifice, charity, and a heart that has sought after the highest good for all people. In short, it is a life that follows the same direction and course of the greatest man that ever lived, Jesus Christ.

Please read this exciting book and be greatly blessed.

Dr. David Yonggi Cho
Founder and Chairman of Church Growth International

YOU
MATTER

YOU MATTER

THE RIPPLE EFFECT OF YOUR LIFE

BISHOP PAUL ZINK

gbl

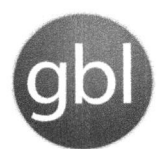

Copyright © 2015 Bishop Paul Zink

Published in 2015 by Great Big Life Publishing
Empower Centre, 83-87 Kingston Road, Portsmouth, PO2 7DX, UK

The right of Bishop Paul Zink to be identified as the author of this work has been asserted by him in accordance with the Copyright, Designs and Patents Act 1988.

All rights reserved. No part of this publication may be reproduced or transmitted in any form or by any means, electronic or mechanical, including photocopy, recording or any information storage and retrieval system, without permission in writing from the publisher.

British Library Cataloguing in Publication Data

A catalogue record for this book is available from the British Library

ISBN-13: 978-09932693-0-1
ISBN-10: 0993269303
eBook ISBN: 978-09932693-1-8

Unless otherwise marked, Scripture quotations are taken from the New King James Version. Copyright © 1982 by Thomas Nelson. Used by permission. All rights reserved.

Scripture quotations marked 'NIV' are taken from the Holy Bible, New International Version. Copyright ©1973, 1978, 1984, 2011 by Biblica, Inc. Used by permission. All rights reserved worldwide.

Scripture quotations marked 'NLT' are taken from the Holy Bible, New Living Translation. Copyright © 1996, 2004, 2007, 2013 by Tyndale House Foundation. Used by permission of Tyndale House Publishers Inc., Carol Stream, Illinois 60188. All rights reserved.

Scripture quotations marked 'NASB' are taken from the New American Standard Bible. Copyright © 1960, 1962, 1963, 1968, 1971, 1972, 1973, 1975, 1977, 1995 by The Lockman Foundation.

Scripture quotations marked 'AMP' are taken from the Amplified Bible. Copyright © 1954, 1958, 1962, 1964, 1965, 1987 by The Lockman Foundation.

DEDICATION

To Sharon, my wife of 48 years. She has stood by my side through the challenges and victories of ministry. I am indebted to her for her love and perseverance, which it takes to fulfill vision and dreams.

Also, to my three sons and daughters-in-law, who are all in full-time ministry and lovers of God.

I also want to pay tribute to my father, the late Reverend Dale C. Zink, who was my mentor. His legacy is more than a spiritual inheritance; it has become the compass for my life and the inspiration for this project.

CONTENTS

Foreword by John Bevere		11
Introduction		13
1.	A Life Well Lived	17
2.	Legacy Is More Powerful Than Genetics	31
3.	The Desire of Presidents, Kings . . . and You	41
4.	Creating a New Narrative	53
5.	The Law of Cause and Effect	63
6.	Your Personal Manifesto	71
7.	Taking the Oath	83
8.	God's Sacred Trust	93
9.	Taking Every Thought Captive	101
10.	What You Feed Grows, What You Starve Dies	109
11.	A Moment Turns Into a Lifetime	119
12.	Guarding the Gates of Your Soul	127
13.	No Regrets	137
14.	Focus, Righteousness and the Senses of a Leader	147
15.	Setting Your Affections	157
16.	Embrace Your Life's Mission	165
17.	No Room for Compromise	175
18.	God's Antidote	189
19.	Life Is God's Test	199
20.	Driven by Honor	207
21.	Your Legacy to the Next Generation	217
About the Author		223

FOREWORD

In Psalm 139, David wrote, "*You [God] saw me before I was born. Every day of my life was recorded in your book. Every moment was laid out before a single day had passed*" (verse 16 NLT). Even before you were conceived, God had a plan for how He wanted your life to unfold. That plan is filled with descriptions of the "*good works*" He "*prepared in advance*" for you to do (Ephesians 2:10 NIV). As a son or daughter of the Most High, you have the privilege of fulfilling your Father's dreams for your life by the empowerment of His Spirit of grace.

The heavenly record Psalm 139 speaks of is about your life, but the story it tells is intended to have an impact far beyond the seventy or eighty years you walk this earth. The psalmist declared, "*How joyful are those who fear the LORD and delight in obeying his commands. Their children will be successful everywhere; an entire generation of godly people will be blessed . . . Their good deeds will last forever*" (Psalm 112:1-3 NLT).

I love that the first benefit of fearing God that Psalm 112 highlights is the blessing of legacy. That really sums it up. Part of the joy we find in fearing the Lord is in sharing what brings Him joy, and the cause of His greatest delight can be summed up in one word: people. Men and women are the crown of God's creation, the ones He fashioned in His own image. Even the life of His own beloved Son was not too high a price to pay to have His relationship with us restored. God loves people!

God's story for your life is about so much more than just your life. God invites you to partner with Him in establishing a legacy of power, redemption, truth, and joy that will last for generations and will transform nations. But for that plan to be accomplished, you must engage with God spirit, soul, and body. Your mind must be renewed and your heart must be set on His heavenly kingdom. The impact of your life begins with the intention of your heart.

My friend Bishop Paul Zink has authored this book to help mightily position you to accomplish what God has scripted for your life. Bishop Zink is a man who has both received and established an extraordinary legacy, and his insights will take you deep into the heart of God. If you are humble and attentive, the words on these pages will lift your vision and inspire you to hope for marvelous things to be done in and through you.

I urge you to read this book with expectancy and faith. Remember that you are one of "*a chosen people . . . royal priests, a holy nation, God's very own possession. As a result, you can show others the goodness of God, for he called you out of the darkness into his wonderful light*" (1 Peter 2:9 NLT). In Christ, you have inherited a legacy of goodness, and God longs to establish His goodness on earth through you! May you be richly blessed, and may your life be a lasting blessing.

John Bevere,
Author/Minister,
Messenger International,
Colorado Springs/United Kingdom/Australia

INTRODUCTION

My father was the pioneer of ministry in our family. That is to say, before him, no one was serving God full time.

My father was not the covered wagon, westward-driving kind, searching for Yukon gold. He planted churches and blazed trails in the heart—a pioneer of the spirit with trails marked not by miles, but by the Church. Seasons were marked by revivals, not by weather. While pioneers of old laid claim to virgin land, Dale Zink accepted the call to pastor and laid claim to real estate of the heart. My father was a pioneer, and I am a pioneer's son. Pioneers leave legacies; and what my father left, I have continued.

I credit my own role in ministry to my father's legacy—to a spiritual DNA that makes me who I am, which he passed down to me and that surpasses even the influence of physical DNA. He was passionate about helping people come to a saving knowledge of Jesus Christ, stood for purity and righteousness, and valued missions tremendously, though he never left the United States of America. He had a tremendous impact on inspiring countless ministers, missionaries, and other spiritual leaders in the Body of Christ. He left these things and many more to me and to others as a spiritual legacy that lives on long after God called him home.

Abraham was given a legacy that began with a promise of land, descendants, and stars—a promise that began with one baby, a son.

That legacy lived on through Abraham's choice to believe. Abraham believed not in the promise itself but in the *Giver* of the promise. And so it was with my father, an ordinary man from an ordinary family, who heard the call and loved his Savior with all of his heart. He was faithful to do what His Father called him to do and he believed in the One who called him. He accepted the difficult, always steady to continue the work.

Now, when I use the word "legacy," I am not talking about estates or inheritances—I'm talking about the lasting imprint and influence that you leave behind as a result of how you have lived your life. As a younger man, I did not think much about legacy, but about fifteen years ago God began showing me its importance. I started intentionally living my life in light of leaving a legacy to my three sons.

I told them, "God placed you in our family. He could have placed you in any family in the world He wanted to, but you're in a family of ministers. Your grandfather was a minister, and your great-grandfather helped establish churches. Why would God invest you in this family if you didn't have a call of God on your life?" I said, "You may not be a minister, but you will always be involved in building the Kingdom of God." This was the legacy I wanted to pass on to them.

All three of them are now in full-time ministry, and just as my siblings and I are in ministry as a result of my father, I feel my sons are living examples of the spiritual DNA God has allowed me to pass on to them as a result of the choices I have made.

It is my desire that Christians the world over think intentionally about the legacy they are leaving to their children and the world—and to then consciously make choices that will leave a positive, godly legacy. In a world of moral chaos, cultural synchronism—where we adopt the beliefs and values of the culture around us—and the loss of core Christian values, your stand for godliness and the legacy that will leave behind is especially important.

This book has been burning in me for years. I need to tell the story of legacy—of promise. I need others to see how it is possible in their own lives. Legacy isn't a respecter of persons. It follows those who accept its call. Legacy's call is for a holy life—set apart. Its call is for those who will pioneer the unknown and fight for the lost and dying, claiming them for the Kingdom of God. I know that for my father, at times, the road seemed impossible. Yet those times produced gold of a different sort, far greater than anything found in the Yukon. It is found in legacy!

1
A LIFE WELL LIVED

My legacy began with my father, Dale C. Zink, who was a wonderful pastor and a true man of God. He grew up in the Midwest, where his parents served as general store managers in Rapid City, South Dakota. During the early 1900s, when the Holy Spirit outpouring took place, my grandparents were some of the first to be filled with the baptism of the Holy Spirit. This sparked a true awakening in the heart and soul of their son, my father. Throughout the years, it has become increasingly more apparent that I had a special call of God on my life—a destiny—and that I was now the bearer of a legacy being passed down through generations of ministers before me.

I had the honor of being guided and mentored by my father for many years as I grew in the knowledge of what it meant to become a pastor. In fact, working with my father became one of the greatest schools of ministry an individual could ever have. The experience my father gained through the early years of faith in Christ catapulted him into a ministry that involved him with the great healing movement, which included such renowned ministers as Oral Roberts, T.L. Osborn, and many others.

As a young boy, I remember sitting in their meetings and watching thousands of people being touched by the hand of God. It put a mark on me that I shall never forget. At the time I did not recognize it, but I was being mentored both supernaturally by the Holy Spirit, and naturally under the watchful eye of my father.

In the late sixties, I began working with my father in one of the largest Assemblies of God churches in Jacksonville, Florida. It was a wonderful time of my life and I remember how the Lord anointed me to lead worship, direct choirs, and minister to youth throughout the city. I had many opportunities extended to me by other pastors to become part of their church staff, and I also considered venturing out on my own to become an evangelist. Yet, there was something deep within that compelled me to stay under the tutelage of my father. Even though I didn't realize it at the time, this decision became extremely vital to my future.

I remember clearly the day that marked the biggest change in my life. One afternoon, my father telephoned me and said, "Son, I'm not going to be able to speak on Sunday." I wasn't shocked because he had become very ill and was unable to function as he should, even though he was only sixty-one years of age. What did shock me, however, was when he said, "I cannot get anybody else, and I need you to speak." I was immediately struck with fear because this was completely out of my comfort zone. I was very comfortable leading worship, but preaching the gospel seemed so far beyond my capabilities.

Then, almost in the same breath, he told me that the District Superintendent of the Florida District Council of the Assemblies of God was going to be in the service. It absolutely petrified me! I wasn't ready for this, but I had no choice, and I spent the next four days agonizing over putting a sermon together. I decided, *Well, okay, if I've got to do it, I'm going for broke.* I decided to be animated and forceful and confident in my speaking. So I practiced motions and phrases in front of a mirror, and I gave it everything I had.

At the end of the service, one of the saints of our church, affectionately known as "Sister Mosier," came up to me and said, "Son, you have wisdom beyond your years." I was laughing inside, thinking if she could have seen me practicing in front of the mirror, she wouldn't say that. It was almost like role-playing—an act—but when I was preaching, it felt real. She was right, but it was not because I had wisdom within myself, but because of the years of mentoring and preparation that was given to me through my father to carry on the legacy that he started within our family.

As I became more confident, I was not prepared for the devastation that would (shortly) follow. My first real awakening took place in 1976 at the age of twenty-eight when, on a beautiful spring day in April, my father left this world to be with the Lord Jesus. Now that he was gone, *what would I do with my life? What would become of my young family and me?*

I had received the dreaded phone call in the early hours of the morning and proceeded to the hospital room. But as I arrived at the doorway, I saw my father's lifeless body lying on the bed, and I froze. I could not bear to go into the room. A nurse, seeing me in a state of shock, escorted my wife Sharon and me to a room just across the hall where I could try to compose myself. I was speechless.

There in that little room, I wept. It was agonizing. Then, without premeditation, the words came out of my spirit, "Oh God, let a double portion of his anointing come upon me." It was at that point I knew I was going to become a pastor.

> **O**H GOD, LET A DOUBLE PORTION OF HIS ANOINTING COME UPON ME.

For the next few weeks, I visited my father's grave almost every day.

One day when I was visiting my father's grave, the Holy Spirit spoke to my spirit and implanted in me an understanding that became the hallmark of my life. He said, "Just as I guided and spoke to your father, I will now interact with you. I was your father's wisdom, and if you seek me, I will now be yours." It was at that moment I began to walk in my own path of faith.

I wish I could say that this awakening enabled me to change instantly, but that was not the case. I have found that maturity is not a destination, it is a highway. My life did begin to change, however, and from that moment on I walked with two wonderful spiritual aids, the Holy Spirit and the Word of God, that have guided me ever since.

The second awakening took years to completely understand, which was the realization that my father's legacy had mentored me. The many influences he had encountered in his life were now showing up in mine. The very essence of his life was his complete willingness to follow the presence of God. My father was more than a pastor—he was a revivalist. He taught me to always expect that a great spiritual awakening could happen at any time.

These two awakenings have caused me to live a life filled with adventures with the Holy Spirit. They are always exciting, but at the same time they have always stretched me to the point of having to desperately cling to God. They have taken me to India, China, Africa, and the Russian-speaking world. They have driven me to study the Jewish roots of the Christian faith and to stand with the Jewish people and Israel. I have preached in the most impoverished nations of the world and also in the greatest convention arenas, on the stage with thousands of affluent business people listening to the gospel of Jesus Christ, some for the very first time.

Throughout my own life as a minister of the gospel, I have been able to carry on my father's legacy and dream—revival in America, with especially Jacksonville, Florida being a revival city. "I Have a Dream," which he took from Martin Luther King's famous message, was the last sermon he ever preached. His dream has materialized into my dream and a legacy that I have been proud to continue, and am now compelled to pass on to my family and future generations.

God has been engaged with mankind by transferring legacies since the time of Abraham. We can clearly see this from the legacy of faith that this great patriarch left to the Children of Israel. You see, God knows that changing the world starts with a single individual. This person can transform a family, which in turn can impact a community. Such a community then creates a culture, and a culture descended from the legacy of a person inspired by God eventually can establish a nation.

We, too, must learn to draw from the wells of eternal wisdom—the *olam* ancient paths or ways of Almighty God—for this is God's method of creating an enduring legacy among His people and even the entire world, and He desires to do it today—in your life. He wants to begin a nation-changing legacy with *you*.

The fact that my father was a pastor and a visionary was no small part of the legacy that began in my own life and one which inspired me to live a life led by vision. The legacy my father left us kids was the example he lived—the love he showed and the passion he had for souls. He built several churches, and the last church he led in Jacksonville was on the brink of a cutting-edge revival yet to be realized in Charismatic circles at that time. I remember many scruffy, long-haired, bare-footed individuals who wandered down our aisles. They had guitars swinging on their backs, were hungry for the Lord, and yet his church received them with open arms as the Jesus Movement swept the nation and began integrating these new people into local churches.

LEGACY IS THE INFRASTRUCTURE OF ALL CIVILIZATION.

Being on the cutting edge of a mainstream denomination was not without difficulties. Not everybody on the Deacon Board shared the same vision as my father, and the politics that arose from having to get a vote on things like the color of the carpet to what type of hymn books we would use could get pretty sticky. In the midst of these nonsensical interruptions, my father had to have the faith to see the potential, along with the grace and wisdom of Almighty God, in order to realize his dream, which became my dream.

Unfortunately, legacies have been thwarted by such evil atrocities as the Holocaust and slavery. If you are Jewish, your identity does not come from the Holocaust. Your identity comes from being part of a chosen generation of people—chosen by the Almighty. The Holocaust was terrible, beyond imagination or comprehension, but that is not your identity. Similarly, if you are an African American, your identity is not in the fact that your ancestors came out of slavery. It was a tragedy and a horrific experience in the history of man. But don't say, "I'm here, and I have this lineage in my life—my parents and grandparents were slaves . . ." That may be true, but that is not your identity. God has given you a mind. He has given you some time, and most of all, ability. You are a mighty person. We have a black President. Don't go back to the slave mentality of your past, or your failures—whatever they may be. It is time for you to take hold of your life. Leave a creative legacy, not a destructive one.

Our Founding Fathers understood this when they set our country's foundations, but too many people do not understand the true power of legacy . . . or that they are responsible for leaving one of their own.

We feel more alive when we know our role and placement within an evolving legacy. We must understand that we are giving life to the legacies of others who have affected our lives. Even more importantly, we are going to leave legacies to those who follow after us just as surely as Abraham did. The fundamental question is whether we will leave a creative or a destructive legacy, and that depends on the moral and spiritual realities we embrace.

Legacy is the driving force behind all human endeavors; it is the power that perpetuates life and civilization. All of us must understand the power of legacy to know how we fit together in His story for His creation. History's greatest achievements are not really about the prize at all . . . they are about leaving a *legacy*.

The Building Blocks of Legacy

I love this definition of legacy: Legacy is the sum total of all action, qualities of character, spiritual belief, and motives, which become an individual's established historical relevance that can be observed and memorialized so as to be passed on to future generations. Legacies that are based upon the core values within God's eternal truths perpetuate cultures and thus preserve mankind.

Faith is activated hope—it consists of initiatives we take to create desires that might have been hidden away in the secretive chambers of our hearts. God is the God of all hope, and outside of God there is no hope. He is the source of all righteous endeavors. Through His providence He distributes opportunities in everyone's lives—the building blocks of a legacy that affects a point in time. We cannot resolve the immensity of the world's problems with a political solution, but there is hope of becoming living legacies that future generations can memorialize.

God created everyone to be a creator of good. You are not an exception. God Himself has placed you within time and eternity to play a role He designed specifically for you. Many judge life by great achievements, but great achievements are the accumulation of many smaller actions that we take over the course of a life.

> LEGACY IS THE SUM TOTAL OF ALL ACTION, QUALITIES OF CHARACTER, SPIRITUAL BELIEF, AND MOTIVES, WHICH BECOME AN INDIVIDUAL'S ESTABLISHED HISTORICAL RELEVANCE THAT CAN BE OBSERVED AND MEMORIALIZED SO AS TO BE PASSED ON TO FUTURE GENERATIONS.

God orchestrates events to take place in our lives, and if we will be aware of them, we can recognize that he is working in small, tiny things that may not mean much now. However, down the line you may see more clearly that God was directing things or making divine appointments to work in you what He needs to. A great example in my life is a man named George Otis Sr., who simply invited me to help him with his radio station financially—but it led to a trip to Israel, where God exploded in me a love for His people, the Jews.

We produce achievements through steadily plodding efforts guided by strong character qualities and held together by an anticipated vision. First Corinthians 9:24-25 states, *"Do you not know that those who run in a race all run, but one receives the prize? Run in such a way that you may obtain it. And everyone who competes for the prize is temperate in all things. Now they do it to obtain a perishable crown, but we for an imperishable crown."*

We have a word for those who achieve great results and leave lasting legacies—champions. It is God's will for each of us to be a legacy-leaving champion, changing the face of the culture of our day.

Legacy of Champions

Champions prevail against all others through tough circumstances and challenges to win the prize they have set their eyes upon. A true champion is one who has a noble and just purpose that he or she is fighting for—a purpose that has a more meaningful outcome than the joy of winning a mere competition.

When I think of champions, I think of people who overcome, like Wilma Rudolph. Wilma became the first polio victim to win a gold medal in Olympic history; thereby, she brought hope to thousands of disabled people. When she competed in the 1960s, the sport recognized her as the fastest woman in the world—but only after she had overcome the difficulties of her childhood.

The heart of a champion is not filled with selfish desire but a desire to make a true difference in his world. The champion's heart is filled with a deep love that becomes his true motivation. The champion believes that he has a mission to accomplish—a mission given by the providence of God. He is not looking for the applause of man but the reward of heaven. Champions believe that others are more important than themselves.

Champions are willing to set aside their personal comfort for their ideals. I think of Pat Tillman, who gave up the glamorous life of a professional football star to join the Army Rangers after the 9/11 attacks rocked our country. Pat was killed in action in Afghanistan fighting for his country, but we remember him as a role model of courage and patriotism—a champion.

Champions invest their lives for the eternal destiny of others. Champions leave legacies. They trust in God's assistance. They receive new revelations of truth, giving life new meaning. Your championship run is just beginning, friend, and as you intentionally choose to leave a godly legacy, you are making a decision to be a champion for the Lord. It may have difficulties, and it may require sacrifice, but it is worth it.

The Essence of Legacy

Loving forward is the essence of legacy. We live in a consumer-driven society, asking what we can get and have from others. But loving forward is instead seeding into the next generation and asking, "What can I give? What do they need?" A legacy of selfishness will leave our children a debt they cannot repay and excesses that consume them. Loving forward conveys the message God did: He loved the world so much that He gave—He gave us Jesus that we might be saved! He was loving

> LOVING FORWARD IS THE ESSENCE OF LEGACY.

forward, and this is the very nature and heart of God.

Every Christian alive today is benefiting from the legacy of martyrs, men like John Wycliffe who died to give future generations a Bible in a language that they could understand. Men and woman who sacrificed for future generations loved forward to give us a legacy of godliness, and we must ask ourselves if we are willing to do the same.

We live in a community of generations. Legacies can be both corporate as well as individual and range from families, to congregations, to cities, to nations, and even to whole people groups. Future communities of generations will hold us responsible for not only *our* children but also the children of all future generations. Remember, one individual life can affect the lives of millions.

The life you and I live is the foundation stone of history. Let me remind you of the wisdom given in Psalms 78:2-6:

> *I will open my mouth in a parable;*
> *I will utter dark sayings of old,*
> *Which we have heard and known,*
> *And our fathers have told us.*
> *We will not hide them from their children,*
> *Telling to the generation to come the praises of the* LORD,
> *And His strength and His wonderful works that He has done.*
> *For He established a testimony in Jacob,*
> *And appointed a law in Israel,*
> *Which He commanded our fathers,*
> *That they should make them known to their children;*
> *That the generation to come might know them,*
> *The children who would be born,*
> *That they may arise and declare them to their children.*

This nation's destiny was built on the shoulders of the legacies of great men and women who lived with an awareness of future generations. What legacy are we leaving to our children? We must instruct our kids in the ways of the Lord in ways that reach kids on their level. It is time to close the door on the humanistic standards of the secularists and their "anything goes" culture. Together we must raise up a generation of fearless young lions who will fulfill the will of God on the earth.

It's time to raise a standard and leave a memorial.

Faith and sacrifice are the pillars that build legacies. In this time of self-indulgence, examining your own heart is the first step of creating the personal legacy God is formulating deep within your soul. Solidifying your life's purpose makes you aware of an unshakeable heart that must be settled and fixed on eternal values. You truly are an eternal being. Every day, in both great and small endeavors, you are contributing to your eternal record.

> IT'S TIME TO RAISE A STANDARD AND LEAVE A MEMORIAL.

In Hebrews 11:13 we read, *"These all died in faith, not having received the promises, but having seen them afar off were assured of them, embraced them and confessed that they were strangers and pilgrims on the earth."* Here you can see the interconnectedness of the generations. This one statement from the Holy Scriptures awakens our understanding of raising a standard and leaving a memorial.

Hebrews 11:39-40 reads, *"And all these, having obtained a good testimony through faith, did not receive the promise, God having provided something better for us, that they should not be made perfect apart from us."* You and I are connected in life and death through legacy.

The forefathers of the United States of America founded the country upon a constitution that would perpetuate the fundamental core values of the Judeo-Christian ethics that would preserve its strength. Herein we see legacy is the infrastructure of all civilization.

Developing a Fixed Heart

A fixed heart establishes a focused passion. A fixed heart is the driving force that causes all that you do or say to provide momentum to your primary love. It's like rearing a child. You change their diapers and feed them at three o'clock in the morning not only because you love them, but you know you're investing in their lives for the future. It was like that for us in founding New Life Christian Fellowship. If I had given up when it was difficult—we sold everything we had to start our first service—we would not have experienced the plan God had for our lives. Or the lives of the many thousands upon thousands that New Life has touched. We had to have twelve hundred dollars for that first service, and at the time, that amount could have overwhelmed me with fear. But my heart was fixed and I was passionate about what God had called us to, and it provided the momentum we needed to build a church that at the time was unlike any other in Jacksonville.

> A FIXED HEART IS THE DRIVING FORCE THAT CAUSES ALL THAT YOU DO OR SAY TO PROVIDE MOMENTUM TO YOUR PRIMARY LOVE.

A true love for God will establish what *He* loves within you. In the end, you create what you truly love. We are all drawn like magnets toward that which brings passion to our lives. God has placed in you a spiritual DNA that includes a righteous passion, a passion that is free from the contaminants of the human ego and unrestrained appetites. As we will discuss, the danger is that this passion in your soul can become polluted. We must be ready to stand up and protect the vision God has given us.

You must align your inner world to the heart of your Father God. You will work vigorously for what you love no matter how difficult it may be. It is vital to set landmarks—targets—that will lead you to your ultimate destiny for life.

You must learn to hold your words and the actions of your heart in check whenever they threaten to violate your mission for God and man. You must always return to the passion of your heart and guard yourself from the common distractions that impose themselves upon your time and energy.

2

LEGACY IS MORE POWERFUL THAN GENETICS

Consider the story of the family of one of my dearest friends, Philip Cameron. When I first met Philip, he was part of the Singing Cameron Family who came from Peterhead, Scotland to the United States in the late 1960s. I remember clearly the impact of this family with their anointed singing, wearing their Scottish kilts and ministering in music and the Word of God. One of the most powerful examples of legacy being more powerful than genetics is found in their story.

Philip's father, Simon Peter Cameron, didn't always serve the Lord. In fact, sin dominated the Cameron family in the form of alcoholism. Philip's grandfather drank for over forty years, squandering money for food on rum and whiskey, and it seemed the curse would continue on down through the generations. That is, until God intervened.

In his late teens, Simon Peter's elder brother, Michael Jr., was headed in the same direction as his father—until one day when he stopped at a little café on his way to buy liquor. While seated at the table, his eyes fell on a piece of paper: a gospel tract, which he picked up and began to read. It was one of those divinely appointed moments when God changed the very direction of his life. Suddenly, the revelation of God's grace enlightened his heart, and he became aware of the bondage of sin that dominated him. It was a turning point in the Cameron family, and for seven years—and through much ridicule—Michael Jr. prayed that his entire family would be saved.

As time went by, Simon Peter met and married his true love. Because of difficult circumstances—being separated from his young wife through the military—and being far away from home, he began to drink. Meanwhile, at home in Peterhead, two young evangelists chose this area to hold a crusade. Each night, as people came forward to give their hearts to the Lord, over and over they gave the name of Cameron. Michael's prayers were about to be answered. First, Philip's mother, Wendy, gave her heart to the Lord. She was so excited, she wrote to her husband, Simon. Everyone was shocked when Simon responded that he would not allow her to be involved in such religious nonsense.

The years that followed were difficult, with Simon's drinking dominating the family. Yet, his wife clung to the hope that God would make a way. After seven years of abuse, Philip's mother, Wendy, now so worn and tired, cried out to God and said, "I can't stand him anymore. I can't take it, and I'm going to give him to you." At that exact moment, while he was working at the wood factory, Philip's dad looked down at the wood in his hands, trying to concentrate on the whirling blade of the machinery. Suddenly, he started trembling and tears flowed down his face. He had heard his brother Michael pray, "God, save my brother, Simon," for seven years, and had watched his wife pray earnestly. His composure was so shaken and, as he continued to cry, one of his brothers asked what was wrong. He still continued to cry and kept saying he didn't know what was wrong.

They fetched Wendy, and she immediately realized what was going on. The Spirit of the Lord then began to move on her as she told her husband that God was convicting him. Instead of the usual outburst, there was silence, which led her to be more courageous. Wendy told him that the Holy Spirit had taken hold of him. Once again, Simon began crying, but he was too broken to speak. But when she said, "Call upon the Lord," he took it literally and began to shout, holding up extended arms. At that very moment, the drunken sinner opened his heart, and the glory of the Lord fell upon him. Simon couldn't stop weeping for three days. His hunger for God was insatiable, and it never ceased.

That was the first part of the miraculous Cameron story. The second involves Philip, who is one of my Board members. For years, Philip was involved with the Singing Camerons, but he eventually moved to the US and established his own ministry.

We have supported his efforts to help the orphans in Moldova, which he and his father, Simon, began years ago. Simon urged Philip to help take truckloads of supplies to this Developing World country where orphaned babies were dying from the cold and from lack of proper care. Every year, Philip and his family would drive almost 2,500 miles from Peterhead Scotland to make sure these babies received the help they deserved, making costly repairs to a dilapidated facility and providing coal for heating, as well as warm clothes. The living conditions were deplorable, yet Philip continued to push through the red tape of the communist regime to save lives. Not all of the babies could be saved, but Philip adopted one of those orphans himself, which has begun a whole new legacy for the Cameron family.

When the girls in the orphanage reach a certain age, they are made to leave. All they are given is the bus money to leave the orphanage, but what really happens is many are sold into sex trafficking. One such girl, named Stella, whom Philip befriended, sadly died before she could receive the help Philip's ministry sought to provide. Yet her tragedy has led to Philip establishing "Stella's House," which is a safe house for some of the orphans to be saved from that horrific industry, gain salvation, receive healing from their past horrifying experiences, and ultimately get an education for their future.

With the help of ministries nationwide and even internationally, several "Stella's" houses for the girls have been constructed in Moldova, with "Simon's" houses for the boys also being erected. It is truly a miracle of God that Philip has been able to push through the restrictions of the government and ultimately receive approval to build these safe houses for the orphans. Philip's adopted son, Andrew, has now married one of the Moldovan orphans, and they are working together alongside Philip to save and minister to more orphans. Philip continues to raise awareness and support from churches all over the US, with media exposure from *Charisma Magazine* and through TV and radio—and even the BBC and newspaper coverage in the UK.

The entire story of the Cameron family is a wonderful example that legacy is much more powerful than genetics. The legacy is living on and will be perpetuated through generations to come.

Dr. Cho's Story

Another example of legacy is the amazing transformation of Dr. David Yonggi Cho, the founder and Chairman of Church Growth International in Seoul, Korea. I have the privilege of being on his Board of Directors and have spoken at several churches in Korea during conferences that are held there annually. Dr. Cho has had a tremendous impact on my life. He has the ability to take a church from 25,000 to 800,000. In fact, *The New York Times* gave him the dubious distinction of being the most influential man in South Korea. Through his ministry, we have seen a Buddhist nation turn into a

Christian nation. Yet, he has still kept his humility. Through revelation and prayer, he has been able to create significantly what is one of the largest churches in the world.

Yonggi Cho was a young Buddhist teenager living in war-torn Korea. These were unbelievably hard times for the Korean people. The country had been ravaged, and many diseases were flourishing. The doctor had pronounced a death sentence upon Yonggi Cho, which was similar to a curse, and told him that he only had three months to live due to tuberculosis. Yonggi Cho was bedridden, and of course he was praying to Buddha every day for a healing. He prayed, and prayed to no avail, and he grew weaker and weaker. One day God led a young neighbor girl to visit Yonggi Cho in his desperation. She prayed for him and shared the Good News of the gospel message. She also prayed for his complete healing in Jesus Christ's name! When he woke up the next day, Yonggi Cho believed in Jesus Christ very powerfully; he was given the gift of faith and was healed and restored to good health by the grace of Jesus Christ. Dr. Cho has preached this wonderful legacy ever since, and he loves to give all the glory to God for his healing, his deliverance from Buddhism, and his wonderful calling to the ministry of Jesus Christ.

Both Simon Peter Cameron and David Yonggi Cho, though from two totally different backgrounds, are living proof that legacy is more powerful than genetics and that prayer can change the course of destiny through a divine encounter with God.

Jesus' Lived Out Legacy

Jesus himself came to act out our heavenly Father's legacy. In fact, creating a legacy in His disciples was His primary method of instruction. He said in John 14:10-11, *"Do you not believe that I am in the Father, and the Father in Me? The words that I speak to you I do not speak on My own authority; but the Father who dwells in Me does the works. Believe*

Me that I am in the Father and the Father in Me, or else believe Me for the sake of the works themselves."

The building blocks of every legacy are the qualities of character and faith that proceeding generations will build upon. The question is, what have you allowed to be your source of faith and character? You have the ability to choose a legacy to follow and allow it to mold your character and guide your destiny. I like to say it like this: "You can choose which rabbi to follow," and I'll explain that shortly.

> THE BUILDING BLOCKS OF EVERY LEGACY ARE THE QUALITIES OF CHARACTER AND FAITH THAT PROCEEDING GENERATIONS WILL BUILD UPON.

Jesus' whole ministry was based upon His understanding that He was the living example of the Father's heart and would raise up disciples in whom He would eventually embed the same legacy of the heavenly Father. He started a pattern of succession for all mankind to follow. This procession of discipleship, traceable all the way back to Jesus Himself, is where the idea of "apostolic succession" began. Apostolic succession is a term for the way Christians have discipled and laid hands on successive generations of followers to convey a blessing in a line you can trace all the way back to Jesus laying His hands on His disciples.

I have participated in this myself during my consecration service when I became a bishop, taking an oath that I would treat all the parts of the Body of Christ as equal, no matter the denomination. A cloak was laid over me during the ceremony, and as I was there under that mantle, something happened. I thought the ceremony was largely ceremonial, but the Holy Spirit came upon me and showed me that I needed to be more of an apostolic leader—a leader not just to my church but also to believers outside of my church. Again we see that legacy is the infrastructure of all civilization, including the leadership of the Body of Christ.

During the time of Jesus, it was common for a young religious Jewish man to choose a rabbi to follow. The idea was not just to listen and learn the teachings of this rabbi but to observe his every characteristic and mannerism. From this practice we get the term "follow the dust of the rabbi." By only allowing the most observant of students to follow after him, the rabbi secured his legacy and teachings for many generations to come.

Genesis 49:33 says, "*And when Jacob had finished commanding his sons, he drew his feet up into the bed and breathed his last, and was gathered to his people.*" The seeds we plant in our children today become the harvest that affects our world tomorrow. To mentor a child is to mentor the entire world, and when you pass on your intimate connection to Jesus, you are in effect engaging in your own type of apostolic succession.

The Essential Components of Legacy

Depth of commitment is the truest test of godly character. Only *you* can focus your life toward a continuous, lifelong objective—no one can do it for you. To establish a legacy, you must ask yourself if you are firmly committed to the vision God has for your life. I'd like to share with you a few major points that God showed me regarding legacy.

- **If you have impaired vision, it will prevent you from establishing legacy.** Within the biblical text, we clearly see that God establishes every relationship He had with mankind upon the highest foundation possible—the foundation of eternal covenant. We know that in the Hebrew mindset, once a covenant was established it became *perpetual*—for all time. That is obviously impossible for anyone but God, showing that you cannot hope to have a lasting legacy without Him.

The most successful individuals in history were those who made a *covenant* with the vision of their heart. It is essential to make covenant with people, but until you make a permanent covenant with the vision that God has implanted in your heart, you have nothing to contribute to the next generation. You must make a covenant with your vision.

- **Conviction without commitment is the highest form of treason.** In this post-modern society, people are easily negotiated out of their convictions. One of today's greatest challenges is a lack of core convictions to guide us as a people. Without established convictions, we will become an aimless generation without a righteous legacy. Without a righteous legacy, we will be become another failed civilization with no sustainable culture.

- **A person who possesses strong convictions and an unshakable vision does not react to circumstances but possesses a focused response.** Knee-jerk reactions are emotional, fear-based responses that leave aside wisdom and knowledge. There is a huge difference between emotions and passions. Concentrated focus guides passions, while emotions are instinctive and intuitive feelings distinctive from reason and knowledge. Wisdom must guide your emotions.

- **Your emotional displays reveal the hidden god of your life.** *Whatever controls your emotions rules your life.* People see what you do more than they hear what you say. Jesus asked His disciples to follow Him to discover the truth of His teachings by seeing the life that He lived. *Mentoring is modeling wisdom.* Always remember that what you do speaks louder then what you say.

- **Ignorance should only be a temporary excuse.** Within the biblical Hebrew mindset, the study of truth contained in the Torah is an act of worship. It has been said that "A room without a book is like a man without a soul." Your pursuit is not for information but for *wisdom*.

- **The waste caused by mediocrity induces self-distraction.** When you fail to take action, you allow strong-willed, manipulative people to take control of your destiny. In Jesus' parable about the master distributing money to his servants, only the one who failed to do anything was considered unprofitable. Taking initiative is a spiritual law of God that brings increase to your life. Your willingness to take the initiative and lead will separate you as a leader among followers.

- **What you neglect will become polluted.** A farmer who leaves his field unattended will return to see it overtaken with weeds. Everyone has been given a season of time to become an influence. The works that you leave behind you are the ultimate judge of your life—what impact did you have on those who follow?

> **WHAT YOU NEGLECT WILL BECOME POLLUTED.**

- **You cannot store time up for future use.** The time that you have on earth is a gift from God that you can use to leave a gift to others. Even the time that you use for rest and relaxation should be done in the light that it will make you stronger for the purpose that you have accepted for your life. You are here to create a better world to follow behind you, one that honors God and His creative people.

In studying legacy, this acronym helped me keep the right perspective and values:

- **L**ove based—If it is based on dead works, a desire for control, or pride, it will not stand.

- **E**ngaged heart—You must be engaged if you wish to connect with succeeding generations, both to God and with those who will come after you.

- **G**enerational consciousness—You must be aware that life is not all about you and the time in which you live and that you will be followed by future generations.

- **A**ctivated passion for a cause—You must be passionate, but also committed.

- **C**onviction driven—Strong conviction is necessary to avoid compromise.

- **Y**oke bearing—Jesus tells us that His yoke is easy and His burden is light, but the world will try to make it feel very heavy indeed if you want to leave a godly legacy.

God has been building legacies throughout history by working through individuals committed to Him, who have hearts fixed on the vision He gave them. He started long ago with men and women like Abraham and Esther, but He has not stopped through today. You, too, can leave a legacy—but before you even embark on that, I feel it is important for you to understand what legacy is from the perspective of the One who created it.

3
THE DESIRE OF PRESIDENTS, KINGS... AND YOU

Who could ever forget that horrific day of September 11, 2001? It was a day that changed the world forever. People in America and around the world were glued to their televisions as they witnessed what could happen when people fixated on hate were willing to do anything to kill innocent victims. I vividly remember the unbelievable horror of seeing desperate people leap from the upper floors of the towers. They plunged to their deaths rather than be consumed by the fires that eventually destroyed the towers. Experiencing these tragedies traumatized everyone who witnessed the terrorists' despicable act.

I remember wondering how we would respond as a nation. Who would emerge as a strong leader in the time of our greatest disaster since World War II? Would the first responders act heroically, putting themselves in great danger to save others ... or would we as a nation cower in fear?

Situations such as 9/11 are the staging ground that builds legacies of historic proportions. No one would ever desire to have such tragedy happen just to establish a personal legacy. Yet on this September morning, which started so normally, brave heroes established enduring legacies that generations will remember.

> SITUATIONS SUCH AS 9/11 ARE THE STAGING GROUND THAT BUILDS LEGACIES OF HISTORIC PROPORTIONS.

Every President of the United States has asked himself which of his decisions would become his legacy. What policy might he establish that would make him stand out above all others during or after his lifetime? We remember some of these presidents for their scandals . . . while others left an example of selfless service to God and country.

Men such as Winston Churchill, who inspired his people to never surrender to Hitler's madness, have left an imprint on our society. We memorialize women such as Queen Esther of the Bible for their role in history. She laid her life on the line to save the Jewish people from Haman's conniving wickedness. These people have left something behind, something we remember even today.

Great men and women, from first responders at the World Trade Center to presidents to history's greatest heroes, have faced immense challenges . . . and have left lasting legacies for future generations. Their decisions inspire us and should leave us wondering what our own legacies will be.

But where did this insatiable desire for building a legacy come from? Did it simply originate in the minds of men? Why has it become such a driving force of life? Is it a spiritual desire? Is it born out of the desire never to be forgotten? Is it possible that true fulfillment in your life will come only through realizing that you have left a legacy that will be remembered and passed forward by those after you?

Let me suggest to you that you can live your life in such a way that it advances the progress of greatness within all of mankind and history. Every life counts.

The Origins of Legacy

The concept of leaving a legacy began within the very heart of the Almighty, the God of all creation. He could not create mankind and leave us to fend for ourselves without giving us any guidance and a method of achieving our utmost potential. God initiated the spiritual laws of leadership by establishing unbroken legacies for us to follow. He gave us the Torah (the Law of God for man, found in the first five books of the Bible) to create order. God sought to keep us from civil chaos and lead to our prosperity on earth. Then He established the desire to be memorialized by living in such a way that we leave something behind—a legacy.

The greatest proof that God Himself participated within the framework of our legacy is Jesus Christ. Jesus' life, lived out before His disciples, was the very act God the Father used to raise up apostles who would carry on His ministry and set the standard for what a legacy really is. We all know the seminal verse of this legacy: "*For God so loved the world that He gave His only begotten son*" (John 3:16).

Jesus made a very profound statement that set the precedent for all mankind to follow in John 14:9-10:

> *Have I been with you so long, and yet you have not known Me, Philip? He who has seen Me has seen the Father; so how can you say, "Show us the Father"? Do you not believe that I am in the Father, and the Father in Me? The words that I speak to you I do not speak on My own authority; but the Father who dwells in Me does the works.*

Jesus came to demonstrate the Father's heart and to pass it on to twelve disciples. It was customary for young Jewish men who were devout to seek out a rabbi and follow his every move and hang on every word he taught. They walked in the dust of their rabbi. A disciple was not just to learn the Torah from this sage. Through observation, he was to emulate his every move in order to catch a glimpse into the very soul of this devoted man. In this way a rabbi's legacy passed on from one generation to the next.

The rabbi chose only the brightest and most observant students because he knew that his legacy would only be passed forward through their lives. This is the very method that Jesus employed, and He taught His disciples to use it in turn to spread His gospel to all nations. He emphatically told them to "go and make disciples of all nations."

Legacy was God's idea. We cannot improve on it, and if you are a believer, you are called out by God to be a carrier of His truth and wisdom.

The Real Secret

With God, humility trumps ability. You possess as much potential as anyone who has ever lived. You are just as privileged, just as resourceful, and filled with great worth. Your future is not dependent upon your past. Education and intelligence are very important in life, but wisdom is a far greater commodity.

> **WITH GOD, HUMILITY TRUMPS ABILITY.**

Education can remain information without direction. Intelligence officers within the military gather information about the enemy, but they provide their findings to seasoned veterans whose proven wisdom and experience makes them able to plan a successful strategy of attack. In the same way, education—information—alone is not enough to ensure your success. You need to know the real secret of leaving a legacy.

If you are a person of humility, you possess within your very soul the characteristic God considers essential for being used for His purposes. If you cultivate a spirit of humility, He will entrust you with assignments that He knows have eternal consequence.

While some cultures have thought of humility as a weakness, within Hebrew thought it is a display of strength under control. Every tyrannical act ever committed had pride and self-promotion at their roots. Pride manipulates and controls others for the sake of its own personal ambition. Without humility, we become competitive and will process an attitude that we must win at any cost.

Even if we have good educations and are highly intelligent and have acquired great wisdom, if we lack a humble spirit that honors God above all else, God will not use us for His noble and just causes.

In Kathryn Stockett's book *The Help* she portrayed how black maids not only kept the house but also showed how their natural mothering instincts urged them to help raise their employers' children. In one scene, Kathryn depicts a precious black woman kneeling at eye level with a three-year-old girl, repeating again and again, "You is kind. You is smart. You is important."[1] The little girl stared back into this precious woman's face, repeating every word. This scene could have been played out many times over in thousands of southern households. Moreover, many of the children raised under the nurturing of such humble individuals looked on these caregivers as the ones who reared them and molded their lives in a positive direction.

Too many individuals' greatest ambition in life is to obtain some level of fame and fortune. They are not looking to impart virtue, moral excellence, or ethical principles that will sustain their loved ones. Fame is about gaining adoration from others to satisfy the ego.

Those who have learned the key of humility can live their lives to enhance a generation of people they will never see. They have selfless hearts that focus on others and never consider fame as a goal. Fame is

---

[1] *The Help* (Stockitt), Berkley, 2011, ISBN 978-0425232200

fleeting, while legacy builders are givers of life and wisdom that will sustain many other generations. *Humanity has built the strength of nations on the shoulders of selfless men and women's legacies.* They gave sacrificially of themselves for the sake of the greater good of others.

We build the foundation of a God-honoring legacy through humility, coupled with using every opportunity that may present itself to bless and strengthen others. Use every available opportunity to impart significant value into the life of others. This is the secret; the key God has given us, which enables Him to use you for His glory.

Destined to Be a Blessing

When you have allowed God to cultivate a humble spirit within you, use all that you have for the generational transformation. Your destiny is to bless. God is calling you into the service of building human dignity. The greatest use of your life is investing it in others. God established our very culture through living, observable legacies just as He established Christ Jesus' legacy. He did so with the intent that we pass forward honorable characteristics that will preserve the family of man and teach future generations about their loving heavenly Father. You are called to love forward.

Observable characteristics of virtue and self-restraint create atmospheres of greatness within a culture. When people of humility embody these virtues and dedicate themselves to creating loving forward as legacies-in-progress, it can change the very fabric of a culture. But it all begins with just one person—a person just like you.

> **YOU ARE CALLED TO LOVE FORWARD.**

Your life and all of its potential (time, intellect, emotion, and energy) needs to be focused on mankind's eternal journey. You must always consider that God has strategically placed your life in time for a divine assignment. Your greatest breakthrough in life begins when you awaken to the realization that you are connected to God's eternal plan.

But most people are consumed with the question of their own personal value within the context of the masses of people on earth. You might call it the "Why am I here?" factor. If that describes you, let me save you the trouble of wondering about your personal value and why you are here. Your search for significance ends today.

God created you to participate in *making* history. God's records of all the events in time are flawless, and He alone may know your unique contribution. But He is intimately aware of everything that you contribute to His creation, and He is involved in every moment of your life. You are playing to an audience of one, the Omniscient God. You need not wonder why you are here; you need only look to your Father, who has created you with rich and worthy purpose.

A Word of Caution

Be very careful of your definition of success. Any definition of success that is entangled with self-gratification will not contain the nobility of a righteous pursuit that pleases the Almighty. He judges the hearts of men.

Proverbs 18:12 says, "*Before destruction the heart of a man is haughty, and before honor is humility.*" We find the greatest example of this within the heart of the savior, Messiah Jesus. For the Scripture says to us,

> *Let this mind be in you which was also in Christ Jesus, who, being in the form of God, did not consider it robbery to be equal with God, but made Himself of no reputation, taking the form of a bondservant, and coming in the likeness of men. And being found in appearance as a man, He humbled Himself and became obedient to the point of death, even the death of the cross.*
>
> **(Philippians 2:5-8)**

God does not relate to human pride. Pride is outside His nature. His nature is instinctively pure love. As the apostle John said, *"He who does not love does not know God, for God is love"* (1 John 4:8). God has placed within our spirits the instinctive desire to make an investment that produces order and civility.

> **GOD DOES NOT RELATE TO HUMAN PRIDE.**

In our post-modern culture, people do not count God as being a valid player in the game of life. As a people we now make the entertainment industry our role model, not the Almighty God of the universe. We are in a battle for the heart and soul of the human race. This battle will play out before the eyes of heaven and earth. To the victors goes the spoils—and the spoils are our children of the future.

In Deuteronomy 30:19 it states that God has the ability to *"call heaven and earth as witnesses today against you, that I have set before you life and death, blessing and cursing; therefore choose life, that both you and your descendants may live."* Make no mistake about it, we are at the crossroads of time, and our ability to recover the core values that have made us a great people in the sight of God may be over.

We are not only fighting for the truth, we are fighting for the souls of our children. If nothing is done to stem the tide, we face a crisis equal to none in our history. The Church must not only engage our youth spiritually, but it must also engage them intellectually. We must arm them with the skills to combat the humanistic mindset that has invaded the entirety of the academic world in the United States.

In order to do so, pastors must be trained in homiletics and, moreover, make it an integral part of church life. The reasons for this are many, but the basic reason is that the Church has failed in its mission to teach a biblical worldview. We've entertained and babysat, but we haven't given our children the skills they need to combat the humanism they face once they enter university. Because they are neither equipped nor trained, they have no power to engage and transform the culture according to biblical truth.

The urgency of this pivotal moment is real, but the method of recovery is as old as time itself. The ways of God are eternal and cannot be improved upon. We must read the Creator's handbook and follow His instructions very carefully. We must all contribute to the recovery process. Orchestrating such a virtuous endeavor requires us all to get in tune and follow the conductor and His masterful direction. From the smallest piccolo to the deepest sound of the tuba, every instrument must be aware of their importance and blend in harmonious order to create this masterpiece called the human race.

Setting the Atmosphere

What you allow to take up residence inside you will establish your future. In other words, your inward nature dictates your external actions. Your words and actions expose the *real* you—your essence of being. What you feed grows and what you starve dies. And what you behold you become.

Isn't it time to study and internalize the virtuous legacies that have been lived out before you? Isn't it time to reform your own nature? It's time to maximize your life and to increase your worldview. It's time to read again—not for the entertainment factor but to expand your wisdom and understanding. I love reading the biographies and autobiographies of great individuals who became the social architects of culture and nations.

> **W**HAT YOU FEED GROWS AND WHAT YOU STARVE DIES.

Remember, you are a work in progress. No one is a finished product. Every day you have a choice to be a bit player . . . or to be revamping the human condition. Which will it be?

Further, you create positive or negative atmospheres that encourage or discourage the behavior of people around you. You can observe the reality of these atmospheres by watching the effect different environments have on people. From the music in our malls that encourage us to shop, to the music in our churches that encourage us to worship, we are affected by atmospheres of sight, sound, and communication.

Perhaps you have entered a room where a heated argument has just taken place. No one may be saying anything when you enter, but you perceived instantly that this was not a place of peace and harmony. There is a spiritual component to atmospheres that emotionally affects everyone who enters them. Atmospheres are real. The wrong atmosphere can turn crowds into mobs; and the villains of history have blinded entire nations by creating atmospheres of hyper-patriotism and unrestrained propaganda.

But the opposite is equally true; by creating positive atmospheres we can turn anger to reason, and the right atmosphere can sooth a mob into a calm gathering. This is why the tone and temperament of national leaders can persuade people to follow in a pathway that will lead them back from falling off a precipice.

Atmospheres are tantamount to the guidance system of households. As a member of a family, you have the ability to create an atmosphere of rest and peace . . . or turmoil and conflict. Future generations will remember the legacies of both the great and the small for how the atmospheres they created influenced their mindsets. From the pharaohs of Egypt who built the pyramids to commemorate their greatness, to the presidents who have lived in the White House, men and woman throughout all time have left their mark on the affairs of mankind. Even though they were mere mortals, they have left us their legacy by having humble ambition to accomplish the vision God gave them.

Your assignment in life is to turn the intangibleness of virtue, character, righteous causes, and godly core values into observable models. You are infectious! You are a carrier of God's plan for mankind.

The idea is to set a standard and leave a memorial. No aspect of your life is without meaning. The Lord your God does not forget a single expression on your face, word you have spoken, or a deed you have performed. When your journey is finished, He will show you the accumulation of your life work from the annals of heaven and will disclose your eternal reward.

God is counting on all of us to assist Him in constructing a God-honoring culture. With God, everything is theological—nothing we do in life is meaningless. Everything is based on His nature and will, which He has revealed to mankind through His Word.

Reading it in the Bible and actually living out God's call upon your life are very different things. How did the heroes of the Bible stand against the press of the culture of their day in order to leave a godly legacy to their children—and to us? Let us begin looking at who is narrating the story of the future and what we can do to be a part of it in the next chapter, where we look at what is required to be a modern-day Daniel in our current culture.

4

CREATING A NEW NARRATIVE

I recently attended a city council meeting where a particular bill was being discussed that would change the culture of Jacksonville, Florida, where I live. I felt compelled to speak in an uphill battle against it, but I also know it illustrates a fundamental issue for Christians—the narrative, the story, of our culture is no longer a match for the values of the Bible. The question we must answer in our Christian lives, then, is, "Who narrates the world?" More personally, the question for each of us is, "Who is narrating the story of *your* life?"

This question is coming up all across our country, and really the world. The particular battle here in my backyard made me think about where issues like this leave you and me in the bigger scheme of the culture in which we live today. It reminded me a lot of Babylon during the days of Daniel and King Nebuchadnezzar, where the Babylonian Empire had stretched its influence over most of the known world and imposed its pagan gods and immoral decadence on even God's people.

In the classic Sunday school story, Daniel, one of the very few Jews to cling to his faith, refused to worship Nebuchadnezzar and his false gods instead of the God of Abraham, Isaac, and Jacob. The pressure for him to give in to the force of the culture around him must have been incredible. His very life depended on how he responded to his society's pressure. And yet, somehow Daniel managed to not just stand up for what he believed in but to bring glory to God by resisting all that pressure.

The king himself, so emblematic of his culture, proclaimed, "*I make a decree that in every dominion of my kingdom men must tremble and fear before the God of Daniel. For He is the living God, and steadfast forever; His kingdom is the one which shall not be destroyed, and His dominion shall endure to the end*" (Daniel 6:26). So what character qualities and strength did Daniel possess that we in the modern Bible-believing church need . . . but may lack?

The course of our society and the poll and interview numbers show clearly our core values are slipping. Fifty-one percent of our evangelical youth think that same-sex marriages are okay, and many Christians now think of the word "abortion" in terms of women's health issues like mammograms instead of the taking of a human life. How far we have come in such a short time! Unfortunately, we are not headed in the right direction.

Legacy Leavers

We must be like Daniel, who was one of the wisest men of his era and was greatly respected by the king and many of those around him. We must be like Joseph, who, while in Egypt, operated in the gifts and wisdom of the Lord and became the second most powerful man in the world, and influenced not just a pagan nation but the narrative of the world. These men left lasting legacies that endure even today.

You will not have the character qualities of Daniel or Joseph or any other heroes from the Bible if you do not have the character or qualities of their Creator. We need His wisdom to handle every moment of our lives, but especially these big questions. The only way we will get it is to delve into who He is and to know Him intimately.

There is a big difference between believing in God and being intimate with God (and actually following His precepts and His ordained order). Even the demons know of God—just knowing about Him isn't enough! People think they know about God—things like that He is love, is good, and doesn't want to hurt people. This is true: He desires that none should perish but that all should come to know Him. He does not hurt us; we do it to ourselves. We bring judgment upon ourselves; God is the one who established the standard by which we are judged.

If I stand on the edge of a cliff and take one more step, gravity will pull me down to my injury or death. Does that mean that gravity is cruel? No, it is simply an absolute standard: what goes up must come down. We do not gain the ability to float and resist gravity simply because society says it would be nice for human beings to fly. When people walk in sin, they are walking in an area that God has said is off-limits because it brings pain and separation from Him. He is not cruel for giving the standard, and the consequences are not cruel either anymore than gravity is cruel.

Know Your Identity in Christ

If you wish to be a modern-day Daniel, you must understand the nature of your identity in Christ. Being born again is not just asking God to forgive you of your sins. Being born again is joining the family of God and operating in the way His family functions. You cannot be a wise man or woman of God and influence culture or leave a legacy until you are a child of God first.

> **IF YOU WISH TO BE A MODERN-DAY DANIEL, YOU MUST UNDERSTAND THE NATURE OF YOUR IDENTITY IN CHRIST.**

Being a child of God is not a

religious thing; it is not about doctrinal understanding. And not everyone who calls himself a Christian is truly in the family of God—he may have a religious belief system, but truly knowing God is not just having a religious philosophy. To know Him, we must be intimate with Him—literally becoming part of the very family of God.

In 1 John 3:1 we read, *"Behold what manner of love the Father has bestowed on us, that we should be called children of God! Therefore the world does not know us, because it did not know Him."* We are His children, but the people who belong to this world won't recognize us as His children because they do not know Him.

Jesus said that the eyes of the people of His day were blinded and so they did not recognize Him. If they did not know Him, they will not know you. If they mocked Him, they're going to mock you. If they ridicule Jesus and what He truly stands for, they will ridicule you. It should not be strange to us that the vast majority of the world thinks true followers of Jesus are way outside normal thinking, because they do not recognize that true biblical thinking is the leading of the Father and not just another moral or religious philosophy.

Want to influence your culture and leave a legacy? Know God intimately, and expect opposition from the world. Then, go do what He has commanded you to do anyway!

Weakness is not Wickedness

If that last paragraph seems impossible, it is because you need help—help that only comes from God and the operation of His Holy Spirit in your life. It is time for some transformation to take place. The good news is, God has a plan. Romans 12:2 says, *"And do not be conformed to this world, but be transformed by the renewing of your mind, that you may prove what is that good and acceptable and perfect will of God."*

Every one of us has some kind of weakness—every one! If you want to be a modern-day Daniel, understand that *your weakness is not wickedness.* Weakness is an area where you have room to grow. When Jesus called His disciples to Him, they were uneducated fishermen. After His ascension, the Sanhedrin called the disciples "unlearned men." However, they did not stay that way. Peter, who began just as a fisherman, was the rock on which God built His Church! They grew and matured as believers, and their weaknesses did not hold them back from accomplishing God's plan.

Weaknesses do not disqualify you, but they do tell you where you need to grow and increase into something you are not. Weaknesses are often areas where we are underdeveloped, but the same way you cannot blame a child for not knowing the things an adult knows, so too does God not disqualify you because of your weakness.

Instead, He sees you as a blank page—and as a blank canvas; He has the opportunity to create a masterpiece with you! Your life is simply a blank piece of paper on which God can author a master narrative that He can use to influence the narrative of your culture.

In the same vein, simple immaturity is not sin. You can mature and grow as a person and as a Christian, and you *will* mature if you follow the ways of the Lord. But immaturity should not be a permanent condition.

People often do things out of immaturity and it ends in failure, but this does not make it necessarily a sin—and failure is not final. You can grow, mature, and overcome, and your failures are not final! That is truly good news.

It is easy to begin to identify yourself with your failures, sometimes so much so that it becomes the description of your life. But I am a living example that failure is not final—I have failed many times, but I refuse to stay there. With God's help, you can be an overcomer.

Fear is Not Permanent

Just as failure is not final, fear is not a permanent condition. You can build faith and confidence. My son Brandon now often plays the guitar at our church services, but when he started playing the guitar, he was absolutely terrified to do so in front of people. I'm not talking uncomfortable; he was completely and utterly terrified! I tried to help by informing him months in advance that I wanted him to play backup with our worship team on a particular song. He had months to practice and would be able to blend in—all he had to do was play along with them. I could've done that, and I don't even play the guitar! However, when the day came and it was his song, his feet were rooted to the ground in terror, and he could not go out on stage.

He faced a decision, a pivotal moment where that fear could have become permanent. We continued to encourage him, but we also did not want that fear to take root. We continued to build him up and his confidence grew, and today no shred of that fear remains.

Most of us have feared something. But have you allowed it to remain? Fear is not a permanent condition . . . unless you allow it to remain. How do you get rid of fears? You must have a relationship with the Father to overcome truly deep-seated fears. Only in relationship with Him and by hearing His voice can you overcome. He will encourage you and build your faith so that your fears do not become permanent conditions.

If you have fears that you have not yet overcome, I would ask if you have heard His voice on the matter. Are you listening to God? Because if you still have the fear and are not listening to God, to whom are you listening? You're most likely listening to your own mind, and if that fear remains, you are in danger of it becoming permanent—final. But with Christ Jesus there is always hope.

Ignorance is Not an Unending Condition

Ignorance is also not permanent; the Lord can teach you, and in fact promises in His Word that the Holy Spirit can teach us all things that pertain to life and godliness. Thank God ignorance does not have to be permanent!

We have a new, cute little puppy—who weighs over one hundred pounds! My wife Sharon bathed her one day, and the next day with her smelling all good from her bath, I took her for a walk. I was very proud of her for completing her bathroom duties, but just a little farther in the walk we passed by a pond and she flopped herself onto her back and started wiggling. I knew exactly what was happening, pulled on the leash, and said, "No! No!" You see, she likes to wallow in duck doo doo and is too ignorant to know that it's just not what we do in our family! As I gave her another bath, I thanked God that ignorance is not a permanent condition and we—and very large puppies—can learn if we are instructed and corrected. But we must accept that correction.

The problem is that we do not always receive correction and often do not want to be corrected. We often resist correction, have made up our minds on various issues, and resist it when God attempts to correct us. The bill up for decision in my city that I mentioned at the beginning of this chapter is a prime example of this, where ignorant human thinking resists correction back to God's standard. Just like flaunting gravity, disobeying the standard will result in injury or destruction.

The Bible says that in the last days people will not want to retain God in their minds (Romans 1). When we do this, we become *reprobate*, which means unable to discern right from wrong. We are definitely there in our culture! It is not just a problem of those who embraced sin, it is also a problem of those who have believed propaganda that makes it sound like that sin is a rational choice. When we resist correction from God, we lose the ability to tell right from wrong. And as we are seeing, our culture has not just lost the ability to tell right from wrong but is reputing the idea that right and wrong even *exist*.

Human thinking, reasoning, and intellect are in no way comparable to the wisdom of God. He is always right! If you want that wisdom, there are only two ways to acquire it. The first is by reading His Word (and not altering it to fit your preconceptions or cultural pressure). Second is embracing the presence of the Holy Spirit, who is your teacher if you are in Christ. The Bible says that He will guide you into all truth and show you what is to come.

> IF YOU WANT HIS WISDOM, BE STILL AND KNOW GOD.

You cannot be transformed without the Word of God or the presence of the Holy Spirit, and you can really only tune into the Holy Spirit when you are in close intimacy with God. But most people do not take the time to have an audience with God and grow and mature in their intimacy with Him because they are too busy.

If you want His wisdom, be still and know God.

Hopelessness Does Not Have to Be Lethal

If you have failed because of ignorance or immaturity, be encouraged and do not lose hope. If you are depressed and hopeless, I have good news: hopelessness does not have to be lethal! You can build a new vision, and the same way fear does not have to be permanent if you do not let it stand, hopelessness does not have to be lethal to your dreams and desires as long as you find your hope in God.

A wonderful verse from the Psalms says, *"When doubts filled my mind, your comfort gave me renewed hope and cheer"* (Psalms 94:19 NLT). The Holy Spirit is our Comforter, and God wants you to find your hope and joy in Him personally, not your dogma or religious beliefs.

You may have failed or have imposing Goliaths standing between you and your dreams. Remember this: focus on one giant to slay at a time. Don't try to change your whole life or world in one fell swoop; pick your battles one at a time as God gives you wisdom.

One very encouraging thing to remember when you are hopeless and looking for comfort is that seasons come and go. You can be in a troubled season of your life, but that does not mean that it's permanent! I remember being an awkward teenager and how difficult it was, and when I do, I thank God it was just a season. In my twenties, I felt like I could do anything—I was taller than a giant and able to leap buildings in a single bound! There wasn't anything I couldn't tackle. In my thirties, I began to contemplate more, to think before I acted and before I opened my mouth. I realized I might not be superman. Later, I knew it for sure! It forced me to trust God.

Each one of your seasons gives you the chance to become just a bit more mature. Seasons come and go, and no matter where you are in life right now, no matter how old you are, it is just one season of life. Things are going to change. *You* are going to change, and you're going to have another season. But if you are listening to God's voice and allowing Him to mature you, you don't have to stay in the negative seasons.

It is easy to envy Christians in good seasons and not think about where they came from and the fact that at one time they did not look so good. But through God's Word and the guidance of the Holy Spirit in their lives, they have transitioned from seasons of immaturity and weakness and have been transformed into something greater than they were before. It's easy to see these people and think that they are somehow special, but God does not play favorites. If He did it for them, He can do it for you.

This comes back to the idea that you start off as an empty canvas on which He can paint a masterpiece. Your life is an empty canvas, and God is beginning to paint. Have you ever watched someone paint? I cannot draw two straight lines together, but I can recognize and appreciate other people with artistic talent. I have watched students as their work began with a bunch of nothing, but a few days later had really begun to come alive. By the time they are done, they are awesome, recognizable pictures of the vision that was in the artists' minds.

You are a work in progress. God wants to take the weakness, fear, ignorance, and hopelessness that may stand between you and leaving a legacy like Daniel, and perfect you by the power of His Holy Spirit. For some, these things have prevented you from feeling like you can begin creating a legacy. For others, you have tried and failed. In the next chapter, I want to show you how your failure is not final, how there is always grace to get up, and how God wants to make you clean so He can resume His master work in your life.

5
THE LAW OF CAUSE AND EFFECT

I want this next statement to set you free: No matter your history of failure because of immaturity or ignorance, when you commit to God wholeheartedly, you are freed from your old legacy of failure to build on a new legacy in Jesus Christ. The history of your past is not the history of your future!

In the previous chapter, I introduced a few problems that make people feel that they do not qualify to leave a legacy or that stops them from investing themselves. However, what if you have tried to live for God but failure or falling short now hangs over your head? Every one of us has an imperfect history—we have all fallen short of God's glory. Whatever it is that you feel disqualifies you, I want you to take this as an opportunity to see that the chance for a new legacy lies before you.

THE HISTORY OF YOUR PAST IS NOT THE HISTORY OF YOUR FUTURE!

From this moment on, I challenge you to give yourself no excuse for staying where you are and wondering if you are ever going to make anything out of your life. First of all, understand that left to yourself, you will not succeed—your weaknesses, fears, ignorance, and loss of hope will pull you down sooner or later.

You may look at people in the world who seem very successful and think that they prove we human beings can make ourselves a success, but I would counter with the knowledge that many people who look successful have hidden areas of failure. They may be successful in business but not in their relationships at home, or they may have fame but lack peace and are tormented inside. We can put up a good front and façade, but God knows the heart, and without Him you will not have true, lasting success by standards of eternal value.

You cannot succeed on your own, but Jesus *within you* can power you to achieve God's dream for your life. If you tap into the right resource, you're going to see your canvas become a masterpiece! It may not look like much right now, but in the hands of the Master Craftsman, you will gain beauty that you cannot even imagine—and a life that will be a lasting legacy.

Let us look together at some decisions you can make so the Master Craftsman can work with your life.

Quit Making Excuses for Your Weaknesses

One of the first things I challenge you to do in building this legacy is to quit making excuses for your weaknesses. You have to quit excusing yourself for bad habits, bad thinking, and bad actions. Do not say to yourself, "This is just the way I am." It's the way you are *right now*; it is not how you should *stay*.

A man from my church came to me to share his difficulties. He was once an influential executive at a big company and had lots of "success." Then something happened, and suddenly he couldn't think clearly or make decisions. He lost his job, and the pressure of finding a new one was too much for him—he was an emotional wreck. After three years, he had accepted that this was just the way his life was going to be. "I can't make any decisions anymore," he said. "I can't do anything."

> QUIT MAKING EXCUSES FOR YOUR WEAKNESSES.

I had an idea of how to reach him, so I asked him where he lived and about the things that he owned. "Do you have a nice TV? What kind of car do you drive?" I asked. He told me he did have a nice TV and a pretty good car. I told him, "Good! Because I'm going to come over to your house tonight and take all your stuff from you! And while I'm there, I'm going to beat up your wife and push your kids around." He said, "What?" He didn't think I could be serious.

I looked him in the eye and said, "Well, you do not seem to be fighting for anything—you've given up. If you're not going to fight for what's important to you, I can just come over and take it." I started kicking his leg a little—he was bigger than I am, so I was going out on a limb here—and I told him, "I think I can take you. You're not going to fight back, and I'm not afraid of you. I will come over and take everything that's important to you."

He started to get angry, and I finally said, "Okay! So there is some fight inside of you after all. When are you going to unleash that part of you again?" He was making excuses for his weaknesses, like so many of us do, and he had to stop it—he had to quit making excuses and fight back.

Too many of us have made excuses for our weaknesses and have no fight in us for what's important. If you have lost your fight—or never had it—your weakness isn't your problem. Your source is the problem! You just need a new resource for dealing with your weakness and to quit making excuses. You need to fight back—to fight for righteousness—

and tap into God's unending resources rather than trying to do it on your own.

No matter your perceived weakness, if you will sell out completely to God and to the power of His Word and Holy Spirit operating in your life, you can be a totally transformed person. That transforming process will cure your weakness, killing one giant at a time until you are a Daniel or Joseph for your day and able to leave a godly legacy.

Social Christian or Sold Out Christian?

I began the previous chapter talking about speaking at a city council meeting regarding a bill I think is directly opposed to biblical Christian values. The thing is, that room was full of "Christians"—but they might be what I call "social Christians." I obviously don't know the heart of these men and women, but judging by their actions they are willing to lay aside the values of the Bible to appease society's pressures. I call that a "social Christian"—they're only "Christians" when it looks good and serves their ends.

And these are the men and women narrating the story of our society. They are Christians by appearance on Sunday, but when it comes to standing up for the biblical standards, they compromise and cave to social pressure. They have let media, entertainment, human rationale, and social pressure set the narrative for their own core beliefs.

Our academics have bought into evolution and removed God from our schools, teaching our children that there is no Creator, order to the world, or purpose for their lives. They are just very smart monkeys—animals really—so they can do whatever smart animals like to do. This has spun out into the arts, entertainment, media, and even business.

Our entertainment is made by a small fraction of our country's population, who do not represent godly values, and they promote their agenda. Though homosexuals (according to hard statistics and reputable studies) represent only a very small fraction of society, our entertainment tells a story that they are a large portion of our culture, that what they're doing is okay, and that to do the right thing, we must accept their lifestyle and recognize it legally in the institution of marriage.

The narrative of our country has moved so far from what our founding fathers intended when they created a Christian nation. We are quickly losing the distinction that has set this country apart from so many others for so long and allowed God to bless us. Will you stand by, a social Christian, and let it happen? Or will you be a Daniel today and fight back for what is right? It's time to answer that question.

Communicate With God

So which narrative will you let set the legacy of your life? That of the world, or that of the Word? If you choose God's story, it is not just about the legalistic understanding of the Word—it requires God's presence within His Word. The presence of God comes by communicating with Him.

The Hebraic understanding of prayer gives us the word *tefilah*. It means to judge, differentiate, clarify, or decide. It comes from a Hebrew root word used in a court of law to sift evidence or make a decision.

The connotation I saw for our prayer life is so interesting: if you are a person of prayer and you are truly communicating with God and reading His Word, the Hebrew understanding of prayer tells us that you will gain clarity, good judgment, and wisdom while in communion with God. You will be able to differentiate right from wrong.

In Genesis, it tells us that God made man from the dust of the ground and then breathed into his nostrils, making him a living soul. The word soul there comes from a word that equates speech with life; it means that God created a soul that speaks. This is what differentiates mankind from the rest of creation—we speak. But it isn't just so that we can talk about the weather; God created us to speak so that we can speak to Him!

Since Adam in the Garden of Eden, mankind has communicated with God, and while many Christians are content to let other people tell them what the Bible means, you have within you the Holy Spirit to communicate directly with God! What God says to you will never be in contradiction to His Word, but His Spirit will help bring clarity and wisdom to your understanding of the Bible. This is utterly necessary to prevent your understanding from being influenced by the pressure of society—and that is what prayer is all about.

> YOU HAVE WITHIN YOU THE HOLY SPIRIT TO COMMUNICATE DIRECTLY WITH GOD!

So what is formulating your view of the world? Is it the heritage of your family, your failures, or the weaknesses you have made an excuse? If this is what you have bought into, you are not a blank canvas for the Lord—you are a finished product that did not live up to His dream for your life.

But if you decide to accept God's narration from His Word and His Holy Spirit, you can be transformed and remade into a life that can become a masterpiece. You must choose to open yourself up to His narration for your life—and your world. How much time you dedicate to prayer and spending time communicating with God is totally up to you. But you possess a soul that speaks, and He is the living God who has never stopped talking to His creation. Our society shows we have stopped listening as a group, but if you wish to leave a lasting legacy, you will personally answer the question of who is narrating your life by buying wholeheartedly into one answer. That answer can only be Jesus Christ!

We will one day give an account of even our smallest actions, so do we go about being good stewards of the time God has given us on this planet for legacy building? Creating your manifesto, your proclamation to the world, is a great step.

6

YOUR PERSONAL MANIFESTO

Now is the time to step out of the boat and launch out into the deep. Choosing to accept God's narration of your life and welcoming the Holy Spirit so you can be transformed is a vital decision concerning your legacy. His Spirit is what empowers change, but you have a role as well. I want to present something very valuable for you that's had great meaning for me.

When you have cultivated a vision from God that is immutable and unchanging—the true foundation of a legacy—it is time to create your own personal manifesto. This is a public declaration of your intentions, opinions, objectives, or motives. For most people, creating a personal manifesto is the missing link between an ordinary life and a life of compelling influence.

My personal manifesto unfolded as time progressed. I have determined in my heart to operate in excellence spiritually, emotionally, and academically so I can impart the most that I possibly can in my generation for the Kingdom of God. I have determined to listen to the voice of the Holy Spirit and to dig deep into the Word of God for wisdom and guidance. I have followed these principles throughout my life and ministry as a pastor. Sometimes it required going out on a limb, or being on the cutting edge. One particular occasion comes to my mind.

One of my greatest desires is to invest knowledge and wisdom and information into the younger generation. Part of that investment, and one of the most important endeavors I had the awesome responsibility of undertaking, was a clear directive given to me by the Holy Spirit one Sunday morning in 1995 during our worship service. As the senior pastor, I was standing on the platform, worshiping the Lord, when I felt an unction of the Holy Spirit that, in an instant, became almost burden-like. Without hesitation, I presented what I perceived to be a vision of the Lord to our congregation—to build a state-of-the art college preparatory school that sets a high standard in righteousness, is excellent in academics, and is staffed with teachers who are called as ministers and ordained into the ministry of a teacher. The purpose was to prepare students academically, socially, and spiritually for their future impact on the community.

I knew unequivocally that this was of God, and the congregation confirmed this by responding very positively. Two years later, in the fall of 1997, the school was opened with opportunity for students from preschool to twelfth grade to embark on an amazing educational and spiritual journey. Little did I realize that Providence, the name we chose for the school, would indeed become the divine destiny for over hundreds and hundreds of students who are now fully prepared for colleges and universities; I believe some of them can become effective leaders in our nation—perhaps even presidents.

I had a mandate from God to provide the opportunity for children to receive an excellent education from faculty who not only would teach, but who would minister into the lives of students, helping to shape them for a future that would in turn be perpetuated. Thus, a living legacy was born and is memorialized in the form of Providence School.

Your Life: an Autobiography

Jesus Christ declared His manifesto in a very concise and yet comprehensive manor throughout the Gospels—here is a sampling: *"I have come that they may have life, and that they may have it more abundantly"* (John 10:10); *"I do not seek My own will but the will of the Father who sent Me"* (John 5:30); *"For the Son of Man has come to seek and to save that which was lost"* (Luke 19:10).

As we age, many of us desire to truly define what our lives are all about into a few vital objectives. Your life is an autobiography that those dearest to you will read. Your life will have a profound effect upon people if you live it with planning and intent.

The concept of "whatever will be, will be" can only leave the impression that you never established something of a noble cause in which to invest

YOUR LIFE IS AN AUTOBIOGRAPHY THAT THOSE DEAREST TO YOU WILL READ.

your life. This will leave your family and friends to wander in endless search for themselves to discover your true essence, your intrinsic nature and indispensable qualities.

Your nature—the instincts or inherent tendencies directing your conduct and character—reveal your inner world. The way you use your time, talent, and energy becomes an open display of the things you truly love. We always strive to create the things that we love, and what you love will consume your time, energy, and talents.

God initiates every advancement in your life internally, within your soul. You can choose what you allow to become the guiding influences of your life. You can choose your influences, but choose carefully, for they will ultimately formulate your paradigm and in turn the actions you take.

You can cultivate your nature. You will become the exact duplication of what you focus on. My friend Francis Frangipane, a wonderful author, coined a profound statement that changed my life forever: "What you behold you become." [cite]

You have probably observed individuals who developed great anger and fixated their attention on the person who abused them (or a loved one) . . . and then ended up developing the same negative traits as their abuser. But did you know you can harness this duplication process to establish positive character traits? You can transform yourself into a person of great quality through observing and adoring the positive qualities you find within your friends, family, and mentors. It certainly is true that "what you behold you become."

Deciding My Legacy

While attending Southeastern Bible College in 1967, a professor of psychology made a statement that changed my life forever: "What you feed grows, and what you starve dies." This was a huge paradigm shift for me.

Up until that moment, I honestly thought that my life was already destined in the direction of my greatest weaknesses. The raging battle for what kind of person I would become was haunting my life. I hated to study. I was completely undisciplined. I allowed my mind to wander at will.

Being young in the 60s and 70s was an experience of extremes. The manifesto of the youth of that generation was not only to question the establishment and traditions of our fathers and mothers but to create a new moral and sexual revelation that would cause the previous generation to cringe with embarrassment. The motto was experiencing life from an unrestrained mind that fully rejected the restraints of society—"if it feels good, do it."

Having been raised in a pastor's home, I also felt the constraints of a God-honoring man who raised his family on the principles of the Bible. I was a witness to the injustice taking place in the South, and young men my age were being sent into a war. It was in this state of confusion that Professor Miller changed my paradigm by saying that what I fed would grow, and what I starved would die.

> **I HAD AN EPIPHANY THAT I COULD ACTUALLY CHOOSE MY INFLUENCES.**

I had an epiphany that I could actually choose my influences. I had the ability to move in any direction I willed. The legacy that I left was not subject to the circumstances of my generation and its dissatisfaction with the world that it inherited. I actually was able to create a life of my own design.

But now I had new questions: Who and what should I now allow to influence my life? In which direction should I go? I saw within my father a man who embraced a life of faith. He possessed a fear of God and desired to do nothing that would disgrace God or his family. Did his godly morality, which my generation would say prevented him from experiencing all the self-gratifying experiences that life could offer, box him in and limit him? Or did it reveal he was aware of a deeper, more noble life that ultimately gives an inward satisfaction of soul and spirit that satisfies beyond measure?

Ultimately, his legacy of a life well lived won out over all the outer voices that were calling to me. I determined my lifestyle by my own free will and choice.

You Are Someone's Living Example

In a small southern town in Ohio, two old gentlemen were sitting together on a park bench when a young man walked by. One of the men, not recognizing the young fellow, inquired, "Whose boy is that?" The other answered, "That's Jessie Grimm's boy." The first man responded, "Well, he must be a fine young fellow then."

The example left for us by those who have gone before can seal forever the nature that will ultimately become our own established character. But we all have the choice to accept it . . . or to go our own way as so many did around me in the 60s and 70s.

Your manifesto must begin with the realization that you are someone's living example. You can pass forward your hopes and aspirations, but it will only happen if you live with an intentional focus on developing your life's message. You must choose your words, actions, and motives carefully.

You are a teacher. How you live life teaches those who observe you. Remember, your legacy is the sum total of all action, qualities of character, spiritual belief, and motives, which become an individual's established historical relevance that can be observed and memorialized so as to be passed on to future generations. How you live life counts.

One of the greatest revelations of my life was when I discovered that what stirs your spiritual passion defines your calling in life. Living without a righteous passion or a noble cause is the utmost example of a wasted life. God has entrusted each one of us with a priceless gift: our lives. He expects us to use them to advance what is virtuous in His sight. So let us begin by uncovering the essential components of the divine calling on your life.

Exactly how do you begin to establish benchmarks of progress that you can measure that will accumulate into a life well lived? How do you set those landmarks I mentioned in the first chapter? Let us begin to explore that by first discussing priorities.

Aligning Your Priorities

Aligning your priorities begins by focusing on the eternal outcome of your life. Ask yourself, "How will this affect my family, my community of friends, and my eternal destiny?" One of the most profound teachings of wisdom ever given in God's Word is found in the book of Habakkuk 2:2-3:

> *Then the LORD answered me and said: 'Write the vision and make it plain on tablets, that he may run who reads it. For the vision is yet for an appointed time; but at the end it will speak, and it will not lie. Though it tarries, wait for it; because it will surely come, it will not tarry.'*

You must start by giving your life a mission statement. Refer to it with every endeavor that you begin. It is true that your mission statement may be an unfolding, progressive work that may need refinement as time goes on, but start writing it now. It is never too early or too late to begin.

START BY GIVING YOUR LIFE A MISSION STATEMENT.

When you recognize your message and your mission, you can then keep your life in alignment for its greatest use. God is simply looking for someone to invest His wisdom in so that others can observe and thereby duplicate it. You do not have to be an accomplished person; you just have to be a willing vessel. No greater privilege in life exists than being used by God to display His wisdom.

Wisdom by its very nature is hidden from view, and because of its great value we must search it out like fine gold. It is an exciting quest, a life-long adventure. Wisdom is so valuable because it preserves the noblest causes in life. Like the proverbial Little Dutch Boy who saved his people by plugging the hole in the dike to keep the floodwaters from covering the land, you also may become an instrument of God, used to safeguard your generation from unseen danger.

You will find that you will have encounters with the Holy Spirit of

God. These encounters are divine appointments with destiny. He will unveil your calling and mission piece-by-piece, thought-by-thought. The Scripture says in John 16:13, *"However, when He, the Spirit of truth, has come,* **He will guide you into all truth***; for He will not speak on His own authority, but whatever He hears He will speak; and* **He will tell you things to come***."*

Develop spiritual ears so that you can hear what the Holy Spirit says. Your own thoughts may leave you confused and with more questions than answers. You can easily become overwhelmed by the constant maze of endless thoughts and options that come through your own mind. But when the Holy Spirit speaks, it becomes a revelation to your soul. He confirms within your heart that which you have been searching for. You must learn to move by revelation, not calculation.

> LEARN TO MOVE BY REVELATION, NOT CALCULATION.

We derive revelation from the wisdom and the foreknowledge of God. Calculation comes from the limited imagination of the human mind. Imagination can become polluted by your own ego and misled by selfish appetites, but God's ways will always lead you into the ultimate use of your life. His omnipotent wisdom is the only true counsel for our lives. Incorporate a supreme aim in your life—this is the only path to true and lasting fulfillment.

Job 28:20 says, *"From where then does wisdom come? And where is the place of understanding?"* Later, it says, *"God understands its way, and He knows its place"* (Job 28:23).

Never allow your current methods and cycle of living to become a bondage. Our comfort zones can easily become areas of bondage—we just get too comfortable with our methods and actions. We do the same things over and over again because we are comfortable there, unchallenged. But when God calls you to do something for Him, it will almost never be within that comfort zone—it will be something that you must step out in faith to accomplish.

For me, one of the biggest changes God called me to was leaving my denomination—the denomination in which my father had and other family members currently ministered. This was the denomination in which I'd grown up, and God told me, "Take that title off your door and just preach to My people." This is what I got from Him after three days of prayer—the instruction to leave my comfort zone to follow Him into something that would leave a legacy He was offering me. My father had passed, but my mother told me in no uncertain terms that she would die in that denomination; my brother questioned why I was leaving. "If you've done something wrong or you're hiding something, it will come out. This is just not natural." He was right—it wasn't. It was supernatural!

I knew all the right things to say in my denomination—all the right language, how the system worked. That gave me a comfortable framework, but I had no idea how free God wanted me to be until I was speaking and realized I didn't have to be "political" within the denomination but could say what He was putting on my heart to preach. I could preach to people who were Baptists, Catholics, Methodists, or Pentecostals—I could just preach the Word. I started to break out of the mold, not always wearing a suit—in fact, we even took one service out of the sanctuary and to a city park!

You must always be flexible and recognize the supremacy of God's revealed wisdom. Aligning your life to newly discovered and proven wisdom will freshen up your life. Anticipating the changes that will certainly follow will bring about a new vision of hope to fuel your dream.

Align yourself to wisdom. The stubborn soul will never discover the freedom of a liberated mind. Bondage is the result of self-inflicted restrictions of the mind and soul. Ignorantly removing God from the equation cripples your ability to uncover the mysteries of life. With God, humility is superior to ability. First Peter 5:6 (NASB) tells us, *"Therefore humble yourselves under the mighty hand of God, that He may exalt you at the proper time."*

> **WITH GOD, HUMILITY IS SUPERIOR TO ABILITY.**

God designed your life to be lived in partnership with Him. Your greatest resource for a life well lived is being constantly aware of the wisdom of the Lord God, which is always made available to those who place themselves under His lordship.

Many individuals believe that the sole purpose of having a relationship with God is their personal eternal destiny. In reality, you are to be living in tandem with God, and together with Him creating legacy. Life is not just about the hereafter; it is about the here and now and what you may be able to contribute into the lives that will immediately follow after you. We are a family of generations.

Back to Your Manifesto

We derive the word "manifesto" from the word "manifest." The connotation of having a personal manifesto is that you are decreeing what you intend to see while you live out your life. Defining your manifesto will help you be constantly aware of how you use your time, energy, and talents. God designed you to be an influence for many other generations that are to come.

Unlike the lost generation of the 60s and 70s that asked the unending question, "Why am I here?" you can live with a full awareness of the reason for your existence. The joy of life is not just in living but in creating. Contribution is more valuable than consumption, and giving is truly better than receiving.

It is important to realize that your personal manifesto is the public declaration of your heart. It is not something contrived to impress others to concede your greatness, but rather its intent is defining how to contribute to the greatness of those in relationship with you. It does not come out of a desire to have a following of admiring individuals but rather from an intense desire to perpetuate and preserve the attributes of wisdom that secures the future of us all.

At the core of your manifesto must be a selfless ambition to inspire everyone with the joy of living in the light of unfolding truth that God alone has established. Life is a journey of discovery. It is the discovery of the intentionally designed legacy we can build between God's wisdom and living an integrated life with that wisdom.

Wisdom is not relative. Remember, society does not judge the ways of God; God judges the ways of society.

If you do not define yourself, others will.

You can only establish your identity by a public declaration backed up by consistent behavior. When I was a very young pastor, I would often be challenged by older, more experienced ministers concerning the decisions that I made. I would often be intimidated and second-guess most of my decisions. I finally came to the realization that I can trust the Holy Spirit who speaks to me. My doubt was really an expression of a lack of confidence in the Holy Spirit's ability to direct me. I personally witnessed how many ministers of the gospel could take on the stereotype of the organizations that they were part of. They would carry the same expressions, even wear the same clothing, just to be accepted within the group. A free-thinking individual fully led by the Holy Spirit was very rare to find. However, renowned people such as Oral Roberts, T.L. Osborn and Dr. Yonggi Cho stepped out of the box, and with God at the helm, would be led by the Holy Spirit to create some of the most influential ministries the world has ever known.

What You Behold You Become

The Scripture says, "*For as he thinks in his heart, so is he*" (Proverbs 23:7).

The origin of your personal manifesto is your heart. Proverbs 4:23 says, "*Keep your heart with all diligence, for out of it spring the issues of life.*" Feeding your soul with positive influences is a lifelong endeavor. You can choose your influences. You can choose your heroes.

You could even say, "What you behold, you become." The greatest influence on your life will always be other people. The life of one individual can change the world. An old Hebrew proverb says, "If you save a life, you save the world." By investing your life in others, you could very well become a world changer and leave a great legacy for future generations.

> **W**HAT YOU BEHOLD, YOU BECOME.

Now is the time to frame that future by creating a personal manifesto and a life of compelling influence. How you live your life will be a testimony to the future, and it may not be easy. The heroes of history passed down the greatest legacies of all time during eras of real hardship. The Great Depression, World War II, 9/11—these are the times that try men's souls. So what was the secret that let these legacy-builders overcome these difficult periods? Let us look at the real secret to legacy building in the next chapter.

7
TAKING THE OATH

January 20, 2005 was a very cold day in Washington DC. My wife and I had received an invitation to attend the second term inauguration of President George W. Bush from Congressman Ander Crenshaw of Florida. We realized this could very well be the first and last presidential inauguration that we would ever be privileged to attend. We witnessed an historical event, something I would be able to share with my grandchildren in years to come.

Washington security was on high alert, and over one hundred blocks were secured off in all directions around the White House. As we approached the staging area for the inauguration, we passed through many levels of security. The crowd had such an air of anticipation! I also picked up on a feeling of wonder about what the future would hold for this President and our nation.

We had already seen the world change dramatically with the terrorist attacks on the World Trade Center on 9/11—we knew that this would lead to the legacy of George W. Bush. How would he lead our country in the aftermath of this terrible event?

We would now see the political fallout from President Bush and his administration's decisions. All of the political special interest groups would be pressuring him to go in the direction that they thought was better than what he had chosen. Would he stick to his principles? Would he do what was right, even if it was politically incorrect? How strong would he be?

We would learn the answers over the next few years, but his legacy was forming even then. He was about to take his Oath of Office as the re-elected President of the United States, and how he handled himself would tell us what kind of job he would do in fulfilling that oath.

We Too Must Take an Oath

"I do solemnly swear that I will faithfully execute the office of President of the United States, and will to the best of my ability, preserve, protect and defend the Constitution of the United States."[1] As my wife Sharon and I listened to President George W. Bush swear his oath to serve our country as President with his hand on the Bible, I was struck by the gravity and responsibility this man would have in leading the strongest, wealthiest and arguably most godly nation on earth.

As I sat in that atmosphere of extreme patriotism and listened to the most powerful people in the world make their speeches, I began to hear the still, small voice of the Holy Spirit speak to me. I could discern it even above all the other voices and the coronation-like atmosphere.

As President Bush recited the Oath of Office of the President of the Untied States of America, I awoke to the truth that *all of us* should take an oath before the Lord—an oath over our individual lives and the role that we should play in His cause on the earth. Something just came over me as President Bush spoke that I cannot easily put into words. I felt the Lord was telling me that it is time for His people to take an oath. We have accepted Him as our Savior, but we need to see

---

1 http://memory.loc.gov/ammem/pihtml/pioaths.html

Him as Lord and take as solemn an oath to serve Him and uphold His Word as the President does to serve his country.

Believers must have a healthy fear of the Lord, realizing He is an awesome God. His Word is not for us to form opinions about; it is for us to obey. *When God speaks, our answer must be, "Yes, Lord."*

Taking an oath to the Lord means growing in grace so that we can become all that we should be as we live out the destiny God has intended for each of us. This grace means that every day we will see another vision of His grace for our weaknesses, but it is actually a higher standard than the rules and regulations of the law. This is not just the grace that redeems us; it is the grace that *strengthens* us.

What I will share with you is not about rules—dos and don'ts. The things God showed me are ways of thinking and acting that cultivate greater grace in our lives, for without His grace and Holy Spirit, we cannot do any of this in our own power or righteousness.

From the insight God gave me there at the inauguration came the ten concepts that I am now sharing with you. Just as the presidents from George Washington forward have placed their right hand on the Holy Bible and vowed to accept their position as a sacred calling, we also must understand that our lives are sacred gifts from the Almighty. We are not to use our lives for self-gratification; we are to live them as sacred trusts from God for everyone to see.

We must be willing to raise our hands and place them on the Word of God, publicly and for all to see, and swear an oath of office to the Lord. You are an ambassador of Christ, a son or daughter of God, and a priest among a kingdom of priests. As such, we can swear a priestly oath to God. Let us look together at these ten elements regarding the oath to which I feel God calls every Christian.

1. God's Sacred Calling

The very first thought that the Holy Spirit impressed me with is as follows: Your oath to God's calling on your life must become sacred. You must consecrate everything about your life to God. Individuals who fail to keep God in the forefront of their lives will devalue their lives and waste their potential.

> **YOUR OATH TO GOD'S CALLING ON YOUR LIFE MUST BECOME SACRED.**

Very little, if anything, is sacred any more. From the sanctity of life to the God-ordained role of marriage, everything sacrosanct in life has been under attack. It is even increasingly common to see our walk with Christ with the same casual light as everything else that was holy and set apart but is now under siege. But the calling of God is irrevocable, and we must treat it as sacred!

You are God's resource on the earth to others. In Ephesians 4:1 the apostle Paul states, *"I, therefore, the prisoner of the Lord, beseech you to walk worthy of the calling with which you were called."* Your life has a calling upon it. Just as in a time of war men can be called up to serve their country, God Himself calls you to serve mankind no matter your religious or secular upbringing. God will hold us to account for how we use—or fail to use—our lives.

The very word "sacred" means that somehow you are connected with God. The more you become aware of God's sacred call on your life, the more you will focus on the eternal value of your deeds. Remember, that which stirs your spiritual passion identifies your calling. Those stirrings are different for each of us, and we will focus our passions on different things. But if we fail to give a sacred oath to carry the torch of God's calling on our lives, we will fall short of God's ultimate and best for our lives. Time and opportunity have a way of slipping away from us all.

Why do we say life is sacred? Is it that we believe that because God is the creator of life we should respect its existence? Or is a life of mere existence unfulfilled without a sacred purpose? Many have come to realize that an unfulfilled life leaves us feeling empty and lacking significance. Perhaps all of our lives are somehow connected to each other's wellbeing, just as there is a connection within the balance of nature. You must say within your soul, "As I live and breathe, I will live for the cause of God."

When I visited the Huguenot Museum in France, nothing could have prepared me for the impact an oath made by some women imprisoned for their faith would have on me. A stone in the Tower of Constance in France bears a single word: "*Resist.*" These young female prisoners carved this one-word manifesto into the stone as an oath to use their lives as statements of faith.

Officials had confined them in this prison tower because they were Huguenots, a sect of Protestants who lived in France in the sixteen and seventeen hundreds. They could have their life sentences commuted and would receive their property and children back if they simply renounced their faith. But the truth that was in them was stronger than the tyrannical world in which they lived.

These believers saw the call on their lives as sacred, and they chose imprisonment rather than betraying God's mandate on their lives. We must ask ourselves if we are taking God's calling on our lives as seriously, understanding that all we do in life is sacred to the Lord.

2. Your Life is a Mission

The second understanding of your oath of office is that your oath calls you to give yourself wholeheartedly as a mission to the lost. You must protect your mission from the uncommitted, for even most Christians don't see their lives as being a mission from God to hurting people. I believe with all my heart that once you are focused on the

YOU MUST PROTECT YOUR MISSION FROM THE UNCOMMITTED.

mission God has called you to, absolutely nothing should keep you from obtaining that goal.

You might ask, "What is that mission?" While we each may have unique visions, our *mission* is the same as that of Christ. God so loved the world that He sent His only Son on a mission. We are on that same mission—pointing people to God through His Son, Jesus Christ. When you truly focus on this mission with the intensity that saw Jesus sweating blood before hanging on the cross, absolutely nothing should keep us from living out the goal of being His representatives on the earth.

You must not form relationships with the uncommitted or those who only want to live life on a casual level, because they will be able to influence you—or maybe even talk you out of your mission for the Lord. You must protect your mission. You must commit yourself, and you must never allow the uncommitted to distract you from the focus to which God called you.

Do not be one of the many people who compromise their goals and even their dreams on the altar of convenience. How many students began their studies to become physicians, lawyers, or ministers—only to find that it demanded too much work for too long of a time? Because the path was too inconvenient, they laid it down for a less demanding vocation.

Compromise is not an option if you have taken an oath. You are not your own. If it were not for the oath that the first responders take to serve and protect, many of our lives would be lost in times of tragedy. They have sworn to put their lives at risk for a cause bigger than themselves, but we too have taken a sacred oath before the Lord that is just as binding.

> **DO NOT BE ONE OF THE MANY PEOPLE WHO COMPROMISE THEIR GOALS AND EVEN THEIR DREAMS ON THE ALTAR OF CONVENIENCE.**

Never build a relationship with the halfhearted. The legacy of the committed builds the future, while the legacy of those who make casual and shallow commitments leaves a trail of superficial work behind them. They leave nothing of substance for the next generation to build upon. If you want your legacy to be more than hay and stubble, you must sell out to God and learn to protect your mission from those who are uncommitted.

3. Seek Godly Discipline

The third idea behind taking an oath of office with the calling upon your life is to protect your principles from the undisciplined. You have heard the old saying "birds of a feather flock together," and so too must we protect what we hold sacred from those who would compromise. We must even resist the temptation to give in to the spirit of compromise in our own lives discussed in chapter sixteen.

As I have said, Daniel is such a great example of a man who resisted compromise. In captivity in Babylon, he took an oath not to defile himself by breaking the Jewish dietary laws and eating the king's meat. Daniel was an academic elite, yet he was so full of godly principle that he put his life on the line more than once to retain his commitment to God. He was unashamed and bold in his stand for the Lord, and that took a solid commitment to discipline and the oath he swore to God.

Self-discipline is the virtue that all other virtues depend upon. No army would win in battle if it were not for the training the soldiers had undergone. You must submit to the drill instructors of life if you are going to be able to stick to your principles. Many politicians advocate the idea of leadership and compromise, but I have discovered if you make decisions based upon principles and then compromise on them—you are no longer a person of principle.

> **P**ROTECT YOUR PRINCIPLES FROM THE UNDISCIPLINED.

Discipline does not come naturally for many of us. However, the

Bible tells us that God has given us a spirit of power, love, and self-discipline. You can commit to defending your principles from the undisciplined—even when that means yourself.

4. Protect Your Morals

The fourth impression that I received while standing in front of the platform where presidents were seated is that you have to protect your morals from those driven by appetite and refuse to be driven by your own fleshly desires. From the White House to the poor house, people driven by their appetites from all walks of life have lost their dignity and trust. When we stand before God and man, we have a trust to keep. Others will use our actions to create solutions—or excuses. We will be held accountable. You will be tested by physical desires and opportunities to stoke your ego.

> **P**ROTECT YOUR MORALS FROM THOSE DRIVEN BY APPETITE AND REFUSE TO BE DRIVEN BY YOUR OWN FLESHLY DESIRES.

Some would say leaders are just people too, and we shouldn't expect anything superior out of them, but not all people have accepted the role of leadership. Excusing individuals from having a fixed moral compass is a slippery slope—and we are sliding as a nation. We need leaders who will leave a moral legacy that is noble and righteous.

When we give in to our fleshly appetites, we participate in a cycle that leads us further and further from God. The more you give your mind to those things, the more they will control you instead of the Spirit of God within you guiding your life. Your oath of office must include a vow of moral integrity.

5. Stand for the Truth

The fifth oath must be to protect the truth from man-pleasers. The truth costs us—it never comes without a price we must pay. Men and women have given their lives to protect the truth from being lost throughout history. Some were scientists who believed the earth was round and orbited the sun and suffered ridicule and censure. Others were theologians who were burned at the stake for unveiling an eternal truth that went against conventional dogma. Truth has always pushed people out of their comfort zones. It exposes hidden and dark secrets that some will pay any cost to keep covered.

> **P**ROTECT THE TRUTH FROM MAN-PLEASERS.

If your desire is for the applause of men, you will become a man-pleaser. Actors and singers, ministers, business people, and politicians—we have all obscured the truth to please those weak in character. But the yardstick of truth will judge us all. Every generation points back to the weaknesses of leaders of the past whose failures enable them to wallow in the mud. The idea that somehow we are all victims of our failed upbringing is an unacceptable and over-used defense—it is an excuse for avoiding the cost of protecting the truth.

Instead of being victims, I believe that many Christians should be stepping up to leadership roles within their communities. We need believers on school boards, in state legislatures, and on city councils. We need people of principle as CEOs of companies, setting right standards and standing for godly business practices.

Even without being in a public role of responsibility, we can still stand for truth. When you stand for something, people take notice. When those around you find their marriage is failing, if you have shown them both love and truth, you can be the one who consoles them and can be the tool God uses to bring healing and restoration to broken lives with the power of His truth.

Instead of seeking recognition from men, it is time to stand up for the truth. If it makes you unpopular, that is a small price to pay for being on God's side. Standing for the truth can also put you in position to do some of the greatest good to the hurting people around us, but we must be people of godly integrity.

Your oath of office to God will place you in rare company when the account of your deeds is passed down to future generations. The revelations God gave me during the inauguration run counter to our culture, and they will make your life stand out like a searchlight in the dark and cloudy era in which we live.

In the next chapter, I want to share with you the other five things God showed me, starting with how to deal with discouragement. When we become discouraged, it can be difficult to stay the course. This is why we must take an oath to God and then trust Him to give us the strength to see it through, and I hope that the next chapter ministers to you and helps frame your own oath of office.

8
GOD'S SACRED TRUST

In the previous chapter, I shared with you my experience in Washington DC during President Bush's inauguration. It was a powerful, moving experience, and during it, God began to reshape my own thinking and gave me the idea that we, too, should take an oath before Him. Let us pick up with the sixth thing God showed me about our own oath of office.

6. Discouragement is Lethal to Your Vision

You must guard your vision from the negative opinions of the complacent and look to the Lord for your encouragement. If you are going to accomplish anything notable in life, you will have to rise above the negative opinions of complacent people by turning to God for your strength.

The majority of people living around you will not be able to relate to your dream. They will not be positive about that which they cannot understand. Most people do not want to do something that will cost them too much—something that is difficult or costly. But it is time for many of us to become workers and givers in the Kingdom of God, not takers.

Your dream is your vision for the future—your hope. Look for allies, but know you will find that skeptics are more apt to give you their negative opinions than fellow visionaries are to celebrate your dream. Discouragement is lethal to a vision, so you must protect yourself from complacent people who see no need to get involved in any endeavor that takes faith and hard work.

> **R**ISE ABOVE THE NEGATIVE OPINIONS OF COMPLACENT PEOPLE BY TURNING TO GOD FOR YOUR STRENGTH.

If you do not follow your vision with inspired action, you reduce it to a mere daydream. You are the keeper of the vision that God has planted deep within your heart. Surrounding yourself with achievers and out-of-the-box thinkers can only advance you toward your destiny. Criticism is easy; accomplishment is hard. Words can inspire, and words can diminish, so be sure you are listening to voices that inspire action toward your vision.

In 1980 I found myself in a very awkward position. I became the senior pastor of a church that my father had pastored before me for nine years. I had been involved in leadership of that church first as the music director, then the youth pastor, and finally as the senior associate pastor. Two years after my father passed, the board voted me in as senior pastor. But in practice it was very difficult for the board of that church to make the switch between seeing me in a lesser role for so many years to seeing me as the lead pastor.

I had no lack of vision, and my work ethic was very strong. Yet time after time I proposed a piece of the vision—and time after time the board voted it down. It became obvious that I would need to conform to the governmental process of the church, which was sapping the very life out of me—or I would need to resign and move on in an endeavor to follow the dream of my heart. With the prompting of the Spirit of God upon me, I eventually did resign and pursued God's vision without anger or discouragement.

Starting over with my wife Sharon and twelve people of faith after leaving a church of twelve *hundred*, I seemingly paid a great price for following God's vision. Yet Sharon and I were able to make great strides toward the dream that we kept in our hearts. As I write this, we have a church with over three thousand members and a K-12 school that has produced students who have received full scholarships to Ivy League schools such as Princeton University. The church has given over twelve million dollars to missions. And because vision attracts visionaries, our church is filled with visionaries. You must protect your God-given vision from the negative opinions of complacent people.

7. Stay the Course

The seventh impression I received came during President Bush's inaugural speech itself. Something he said triggered the understanding that he would have to face down people who would try to use their influence for their own benefit.

We must fight to protect our liberty from controllers and manipulators. Strong-willed controllers and manipulators who want to use your time, energy, and talent for their own benefit will challenge you and your vision. Of course you may choose to be involved in someone else's vision, but some of these people will try to coerce you and move you off center from your calling.

You must stay on the course God's vision sets for you. You are the captain of your ship, and your crew will be all who choose to follow in the wake of the legacy that you have left for them.

> YOU MUST STAY ON THE COURSE GOD'S VISION SETS FOR YOU.

Legacies can be both corporate and individual. You may have a strong desire to be a part of something far bigger than standing alone, but it must be because you consciously choose to be a part of it, not because you were coerced or manipulated. I have joined in with great leaders who have taken on mammoth tasks—tasks that have stirred my soul to action—but I identified with their cause and it resonated in my own heart.

Since there are many aspects in life that demand a unified vision and many contributors, you may indeed become part of a wonderful group of people in a vision that is too big for any one person to fulfill.

8. Pursue Proven Companions

The eighth idea that came to me regarding our own oath of office is that you must empower your vision by surrounding it with committed and proven people. Love without loyalty is not love. Individuals who love their president's ideals fill the cabinet of any presidency.

People of like heart and mind can help catapult you toward victory. One of the themes that I have lived by is "staff your weakness." But you must make sure that you are not compromising by substituting talented people for *loyal* people who share your vision. Surround yourself with people who have proven themselves to be of like-minded, godly commitment.

> EMPOWER YOUR VISION BY SURROUNDING IT WITH COMMITTED AND PROVEN PEOPLE

How do we become proven? When you are man or woman enough to do what is right, you are proving yourself. When you no longer just attend church for what you can receive but become a minister of the gospel to those around you, you are proving yourself in God's Kingdom. These are the things that prove we are His disciples, and people who are doing this as well are the proven ones with which we must surround ourselves.

One of the most trustworthy sayings I have found is in Proverbs 29:18 (KJV): "*Where there is no vision, the people perish.*" But we can also say that without a *people* the vision will perish. Nothing of great substance can ever be achieved without proven allies.

9. Embrace Wise Counsel

The ninth thing God showed me was that we should receive the counsel of people with like principle and character. You will find that it is imperative to find and spend time with individuals who carry the same core values that you possess.

Jesus talked of this precept in Matthew 12:25 (NASB) when He said, "*Any kingdom divided against itself is laid waste; and any city or house divided against itself will not stand.*" The place of agreement is the place of power. Ask yourself this question: Is the counsel you seek merely a tactic, or is it based upon

> **F**IND AND SPEND TIME WITH INDIVIDUALS WHO CARRY THE SAME CORE VALUES THAT YOU POSSESS.

principles and characteristics that are just and morally right? Is your objective to win—or is it to walk out righteousness and justice? You must surround yourself with the council of the wise.

The sages of the Hebrew culture, which is the culture of the Bible, were referred to as *talmidei chachamin,* which translated means "student of the wise." Wisdom will always create transcendent success, for it is not trying to "win." It is trying to establish a proven truth.

Truth is greater than success, and success without truth will become a fleeting pleasure. Anything you produce outside of godly principle and virtuous character will ultimately diminish into an embarrassing failure. You must therefore seek out the counsel of the principled and those strong in character as resources of wisdom.

It is easy to find individuals who are willing to give their opinion, but remember what the wisdom of the Scriptures say: "*A fool finds no pleasure in understanding but delights in airing his own opinions*"

(Proverbs 18:2 NIV). The Word also tells us, *"Plans succeed through good counsel; don't go to war without wise advice"* (Proverbs 20:18 NLT).

Not all counsel and "words from God" that people may give you are really from Him. You must judge them by their fruit. Are they people of like principle, proven to be doers of the Word and not hearers only? Are they uncompromising and unshakable in their faith? These are the people from which we should receive counsel!

10. ESP—Extra Spiritual Perception

The tenth revelation of the oath you take to establish your calling in life is to become a leader who seeks guidance from the Lord through His Word and His Spirit. Seek God's wisdom with great diligence. God the Creator's ways and thoughts are unfathomable to our rational minds, and we can only see them through spiritual perception. I am not talking about the so-called "extra sensory perception"—I'm speaking about developing your extra *spiritual* perception. This is a capacity God has given believers that enables us to receive the instruction and counsel of God.

> **B**ECOME A LEADER WHO SEEKS GUIDANCE FROM THE LORD THROUGH HIS WORD AND HIS SPIRIT

We receive this from God in a few different ways, but most notable is that we receive such instruction directly from the Word of God. Be a person of the Word, who opens the Bible and reads it with prayer and understanding every day. If you lack understanding, pray and ask God for wisdom—but keep reading.

Jesus taught on the Person of the Holy Spirit and how He could lead us, saying, *"However, when He, the Spirit of Truth, has come, He will guide you into all truth; for He will not speak on His own authority, but whatever He hears He will speak; and He will tell you things to come"* (John 16:13).

God desires to guide our affairs with His counsel. The two sources of God's counsel are the Holy Scriptures and the spiritual revelation we receive from His Holy Spirit. The spiritual laws found within God's Word should back up every endeavor of your life.

The spiritual revelation that I refer to is the insight and wisdom that comes spontaneously from outside your realm of experience and knowledge by the agent of the Holy Spirit Himself. Have you ever had a truth or insight that seemed to drop into your mind seemingly out of nowhere? The Spirit of God can interact with the heart and mind of any believer, and God desires to lead you by His Spirit—this shows that we are His children.

Live Out God's Sacred Trust

All of us should take an oath before the Lord—an oath to protect that which He has given to us: our vision, dream, or legacy. Your life is a mission that you will not be able to fulfill if you do not receive the Holy Spirit's power and discipline for your life. You will have to protect your morals and principles from discouragement that would seek to destroy the vision God has given you and stay the course, even when all around you go another way.

You will need the support of proven, like-minded people and to embrace wise, godly counsel, but no amount of counsel is a substitute for the Counselor, the Holy Spirit. If you learn to listen to Him and be guided by eternity, you will be able to live a life that treats God's call as a sacred gift.

When we accept the Lord Jesus, we are taking an oath to live no longer for our own gratification. We are publicly stating at salvation and baptism that our lives are sacred trusts for all to see, and this is an oath of office we must all take seriously, for it will determine the type of legacy we leave behind as surely as that of any president.

Someday we will give an account to God. Friend, Jesus has

redeemed you for a purpose, and part of that is a leadership role that you share with every believer in the Body of Christ. It is a great and sacred trust, as surely as leading the greatest country in the world. But we represent a country not made with human hands and a kingdom that is far greater than any that has ever existed. It is in serving this kingdom, the Kingdom of God, to which we are called to swear an oath. I pray that God gives you the grace to uphold this oath and serve, preserve, and protect the calling of God on your life.

9
TAKING EVERY THOUGHT CAPTIVE

If you have ever lived in a major metropolitan or industrial area, you may be familiar with pollution—it turns our blue skies brown with smog and clogs our clear lakes and rivers with stinking debris. It may take the form of devastated areas where industries have not cleaned up after themselves, or it may look like garbage strewn by the roadside or swirling in the currents of our oceans. Our air, water, and soil can all become polluted if we are not careful and act responsibly.

But did you know that even as a Christian, your *soul* can become polluted? Garbage or chemicals may pollute our land, but your soul can be polluted by the images you see, the things you hear, and the material you read. Pollution of the soul can also take the form of the thoughts you allow in and the perceptions you've developed.

Your soul is that part of you from which your thoughts, will, and emotions originate, a distinct part of you together with your spirit and your body. The Bible is very clear that our flesh, our body, is born with a sin nature and wars against our spirit. Our spirits are redeemed when we come to Christ, but our souls—our souls are either being redeemed and washed by the Word or being contaminated and destroyed by pollutants.

Here is something very important that I have stressed throughout this book: you have a choice of what happens to your soul. You can allow your mind, your will, and your emotions to be controlled and influenced by two things—this world and its "god" or by the Spirit of Jesus Christ. So which are you choosing? Do you even know? You may be surprised by how many believers have not considered this—or who are deceived.

Propaganda

I have noticed something very distressing in my years of ministry: most Christians live in a state of deception. They have been mislead or are misleading themselves about what is true about God, the world around them, and themselves. They have often bought into *propaganda*.

I have visited the Holocaust Museum in Washington DC, and some things really stayed with me. One was a brochure I picked up called *The State of Deception: The Power of Nazi Propaganda*. Before there were bullets being fired in World War II and before the Nazis committed atrocities, Hitler and his followers were producing propaganda to fight a war for the minds and perceptions of the German people.

You see, propaganda uses incomplete truths, or half-truths, and omits information selectively so it does not give you the full, correct picture. It oversimplifies complex issues or ideas and misleads or downplays the real issues, and it advertises for a cause, attacks opponents, and targets certain types of people or audiences. It is specifically created to mislead and to fight a war of the mind, and Adolf Hitler used it to desensitize the German people and convince them that God's people, the Jews, were not really human at all.

How could people have let the horrors of the Holocaust happen to fellow humans? They had been brainwashed into thinking they were less than human, that they were evil. Hitler completely turned what is right on its head, and because he won the war of the mind first, few in Germany stood against him.

Hitler was not the only master of propaganda in our world—the accuser of the brethren, satan, our enemy, is the undisputed *master* of propaganda, and he has created an entire world of it to fill and pollute your mind. Many Christians have become so polluted that they do not even know the level of their own deception and desensitization, and the devil has used this war of the mind to get away with horrible atrocities—while Christians stand by and few do anything to show Christ to their world or even to halt the pollution of their own souls.

The good news is that no matter how long the devil has had his way with the war of the mind, if you are in Christ, you have access to His Holy Spirit and can have your mind renewed and be washed in the water of the Word. You can take control of what is going into your soul and determine to entertain only what is true, noble, right, pure, lovely, and admirable.

Some of you may read this and wonder if there is any hope for someone unless they have walked with God from birth or an early age. It is true that the devil does target our children early so that he can infiltrate their minds in the formative years before they become adults. It may be true that you have been subject to his propaganda for a very long time and thus have a polluted soul—but the great hope for us is Christ and the fact that He has not left us alone and subject to the devil and his forces! Our hope is in Jesus Christ, and no matter how long you have been away from Him and how polluted your thoughts, will, and emotions may be, it is never too late to cease being conformed by this world and begin being transformed by the renewing of your mind (see Romans 12:2)!

Subjective or Objective?

We live in an age when many have rejected the idea of objective truth—truth that is absolute. Most people think that truth is relative—what may be true for you may not be true for me. Even many Christians have come to accept this idea—but it is a form of propaganda the devil has masterfully seeded in our culture to deceive many.

You might think it is easy for writers and preachers to say that if it does not agree with God's Word, which is absolute truth, then it is not right; but for ordinary people living daily lives, using the Bible as an objective standard can get you labeled an intolerant religious fanatic. See what happens when you tell your co-workers you won't do something because the Bible says it's wrong and see how the vast majority of people—even Christians!—respond. They are deceived and have lost sight of the truth.

It is time to recapture the truth.

God's Word does not change, and while we are no longer under the Law and are under grace, God's plan for humankind and His standard of right and wrong, good and evil are just as applicable today as when men wrote them under the inspiration of the Holy Spirit. The Torah, the Law, is *instruction that hits the mark*. It is on target every time. Adultery, murder, idolatry, and all the rest are still objectively wrong, no matter the extenuating circumstances.

We can either judge truth from the narrative of God's Word, which changes not, or we can do so from the world's system and the ever-shifting philosophies of men. But only God's way leads to a life of integrity and a lasting legacy of godliness. The abiding standard for our lives must start and end with God's Word and His ways, for no other standard of living will provide a way of judging what to allow into your soul.

Your Life is a Product

What makes you who you are? What did it take to get you where you are today, either mired in pollution or striving for godliness? I would like to offer a few observations.

The first is that your life is a product of the things you have observed. When we are children, two things influence us more than anything else: what we see our parents do, and our entertainment. Guess which one is often the greater influence on children today—entertainment! As children, we mimic the words and deeds of our parents and primary caregivers, and we also absorb the propaganda of the entertainment we watch. The first influences on your life come mostly from these two categories, and even as adults, our lives are the products of what we have allowed in and observed.

I advocate an annual media fast at the church I pastor—for one month, we have a Take Every Thought Captive fast, and we turn off *all* secular media and replace it with spiritually healthy and uplifting input. We spend just thirty days taking back the territory that propaganda has infiltrated, and we examine our hearts, thoughts, and motives so that God can more clearly show us where we have been deceived. If you have never tried this, you will be amazed what even a few days of fasting propaganda will do to your perceptions and level of desensitization! I cannot recommend a fast like this highly enough, and the longer you fast the propaganda of the enemy, the more clearly you will be able to see it for what it is as the pollution is cleared from your soul.

What we hear, read, or otherwise receive is a huge influence on us. What we observe infiltrates and influences our souls, no matter the filters we try to impose to screen out what we find objectionable. When you remove or regulate those sources of input, God has open ground to work with to clear away the pollution of your soul so you can perceive Him and His standards more clearly.

What we observe is very important, but "spiritual" influences (good or evil) also have a huge impact on your life. It amazes me that some people—even some "Christians"—think there is no devil, that he's just metaphorical, and that there is no hell or forces of evil. They are in denial that their lives can be influenced by a very real unseen world about which we must be aware.

In the beginning, there was no evil until the devil brought it about. Even though all evil originated from Satan, all influences and temptations may or may not be direct results of the devil. However, the Bible clearly states he is our enemy, our tempter, and our accuser.

A good example of an evil influence that can impact your life dramatically is pornography. A person who is addicted to pornography may think he is hurting no one but himself, but in reality he is opening himself *and his family* to the influence of an unclean spirit. You may think you are doing something in secret and that no one knows, but the spiritual impact spreads far beyond you in the spiritual, for you are tapping into a satanic influence that will poison you and every relationship in your family if you allow that virulent pollution into your soul.

"Spiritual" influences can act to pull you down, so it is vital that you make the things of God the greatest spiritual influence on your life. Remember, if you are not taking your spiritual enemy seriously, he can blindside you—we are not to be ignorant of his schemes. However, greater is He who is in us than he that is in this world, and when you seek to cut off spiritual pollution and instead be renewed by God's Spirit and His Word, Jesus' blood will wash you white as snow.

So your life is a product of what you have observed and spiritual influences, but it is also a result of the soul ties that are attached to you—and these can be some of the strongest influences we deal with. Soul ties are the relationships we have with people, organizations, and religious orders—your *oikos*, or the entirety of people that surround you. We may call soul ties by different names like peer pressure or codependency, but these bonds attach themselves to your mind, your will, and your emotions and pull on you relentlessly. You are bound to them if you do not get unhealthy ties broken, and if you are not careful, they can pull you down and heavily influence your life.

Your life is also a product of the habits you allow to stand. You can have good habits, but in the area of soul pollution, far more often the influence is from negative habits we have allowed to remain instead of breaking them with the power of the Holy Spirit. If you allow bad habits to stand, they can come to control you. You may think they're minor, things like eating Twinkies or too many Krystal burgers, but no matter the gravity of the habit, bad ones can create life behaviors that will keep your soul polluted when the Lord would have you a clean and spotless bride for His Son.

They say it takes twenty-one repetitions to create a new habit, and breaking old ones can be very difficult. However, we know we can do all things through Christ, so why not commit to breaking your bad habits and to creating new ones that restore and refresh your soul?

The last factor influencing who you are I'd like to bring to your attention is your image of yourself. Whether you realize it or not, you see yourself in a particular way, and for some it's a real fantasy! We men especially can look at the pot-bellied image in the mirror and somehow manage to see a six-pack or the remaining hints of our physical prime.

Joking aside, the image you create of yourself can control you, telling you what you can and cannot do while what you think about yourself should be what the Lord says. For some an image problem may be that you see yourself negatively—as weak, inept, powerless, or a victim. We may see ourselves only through the deceptions that we have allowed to stand and not as the Lord sees us at all.

> THE IMAGE YOU CREATE OF YOURSELF CAN CONTROL YOU

The *only* way to combat all of these things that have constructed our lives is a proper source for who you are and *should* be—God's

Word, what He says about you, and how He sees you. The Word of God says you are a child of the Most High. You are a joint heir with Christ Jesus. You are someone who can do all things through Christ who strengthens you. You are the head and not the tail, above and not beneath. God's promises for you are good and full of power and freedom.

If you do not go to God's Word as your source, all of the things I have mentioned above will be the dominant forces that control what your life is like. They will control who you are, and you will be unable to cut off the flow of pollution into your soul. This is why you must take every thought captive, and you must bring all the external and internal influences on your mind, will, and emotions into subjection to Christ Jesus.

All of these things but the Word of God are propaganda, and if you are like every other human on the face of the earth, you have allowed the devil to use half-truths, selective information, oversimplified ideas, and misdirection to attack you and weigh down your soul with crushing pollution that can give him victory in the war for your mind. So how do we fight back? Let's take a look in the next chapter.

10
WHAT YOU FEED GROWS, WHAT YOU STARVE DIES

In the previous chapter, we looked at soul pollution—the very real problem that all of us face in this era where propaganda abounds and truth seems to be in recession and relative. But understanding that we are exposed to propaganda and probably have some level of pollution in our lives is just one step; the next is what to do about it.

Proverbs 23:7 says, *"For as he thinks in his heart, so is he."* Some have said that this means that you are what you think, but I think a better way to look at it is to remember that what you feed grows, but what you starve dies. The first thing to understand about fighting back in this war for your mind is that you can choose your thoughts, and those thoughts set the direction for your life.

You are not automatically your thoughts—were that true, every sinful temptation or thought, whether or not you entertain or act on it, would be counted against us. However, if you have ever had a negative thought that you rejected and did not act upon, you know this is not the case. You are not your thoughts, but those thoughts that you *dwell upon* or act upon—those that you allow to remain—will shape the direction of your life. What you think today, you will experience tomorrow.

This concept is important to grasp in the context of propaganda that we have been covering, because if you allow those things to stand, you are allowing that pollution to set the course of your life. On the other hand, if your thoughts are on God's Word, His promises, and His view of you, His thoughts become your thoughts.

An old song we sang in my church asked, "Whose report shall you believe?" The chorus answered, "We will believe the report of the Lord."[1] Quoting the prophet Isaiah, Paul writes, "*LORD, who has believed our report?*" and then immediately states, "*So then faith comes by hearing, and hearing by the word of God*" (Romans 10:16,17). You face many reports daily—negative reports on economics, relationships, politics and more, which may be propaganda—contrasted with reports from the Lord, which build your faith. His Word defies many of these reports; it says such things as God desires we prosper in all things, even as our souls prosper and that no weapon formed against you will prosper.

Which will you choose to dwell on and believe? One will lead to doubt and disillusionment. The other will yield faith as you hear the Word of God and His reports.

Meditation is Not a Bad Word

Too many Christians only take their Bibles to church simply as a custom. They are not opening it up to get God's reports, and they are not replacing the world's soul-polluting propaganda with it on a daily basis. Is where our lives are headed any wonder when we do this? We dwell on the negatives in the news, but we do not spend time meditating on God's Word.

---

[1] *Whose report shall you believe* (Kenoly), from the album *Lift Him Up*, Integrity's Hosanna! Music, 1991

Some eastern mystics might want you to think that meditation is a thing of their religions, but if anything, we Christians are to be the ones meditating—on God's reports! Psalms 19:14 says, *"Let the words of my mouth and the meditation of my heart be acceptable in Your sight, O LORD, my strength and my Redeemer."* This is David's way of saying he understands he must allow God's reports to stand.

The word *meditation* in the Bible is the same word that the Hebrews used for *mutter*, and it means that they mutter the Word of God. They are not just thinking on it, they are literally muttering His Word in their prayers. They do not simply read the Torah, their lips move as they meditate on God's promises and reports over and over. The Jews may understand something better than we do: we must reinforce the Word in our minds repeatedly, because we human beings *leak*. We must start our children early, because the propaganda is so strong we simply cannot wait while they get older before we start teaching them God's Word.

So many Christians just offer *shallow repentance*—saying we're sorry for sins without truly repenting and gaining victory by allowing the Word of God to transform our minds. They think grace simply makes God overlook their sins and polluted souls. In fact, the transforming work of grace is not just to save us from our sins but is an ongoing remaking of our souls into the shape of the One in whose image we were made and who we behold, as through a mirror, when we look into the Word. We do not have to remain the ugly old things we are, polluted and corrupted by the devil's propaganda; we can be transformed, experience God's metamorphosis, and be changed from glory to glory.

We should be praying David's prayer daily—let the words of our mouths and the meditation of our hearts be pleasing to you, God! We should be praying every morning that the Holy Spirit will empower us to take every thought captive and make it obedient to Christ (see 2 Corinthians 10:5).

Every day you face a question of what you will allow to stand in your mind—will it be God who influences your thoughts and the direction of your life, or will it be your enemy's propaganda?

No Negative Thoughts in God's Mind

Many people with an incorrect view of God—they have bought into the enemy's propaganda—think He is a vengeful, smiting deity, just waiting for them to mess up so He can smash them. But do you know that there are no negative thoughts in the mind of God? Even His judgments are good and positive! Just a few verses before the quote from David we read a moment ago, he wrote, "*The judgments of the LORD are true and righteous altogether*" (Psalms 19:9).

When my mother was passing away, I often heard her quoting a Scripture that she had quoted to us as kids—muttering in a way very much like the meditation I describe above. When you are dying, the most important things rise to the top, and the rest falls away as irrelevant. And as her faith was encapsulated into a single prayer, she prayed Philippians 4:8 over and over:

> **THERE ARE NO NEGATIVE THOUGHTS IN THE MIND OF GOD?**

> *Finally, brethren, whatever things are true, whatever things are noble, whatever things are just, whatever things are pure, whatever things are lovely, whatever things are of good report, if there is any virtue and if there is anything praiseworthy—meditate on these things.*

What we allow to stand in our minds is so incredibly important. Negativity should have no place in our thoughts, and neither should complaining. God took Israel's complaints so seriously that He waited while an entire generation died off in the wilderness before He allowed their children to enter the Promised Land—that should tell us something about how God views negativity and complaining.

Instead, we should embrace the fact that Psalms 100:4 is not just poetic but a mandate for our thoughts: "*Enter into His gates with thanksgiving, and into His courts with praise. Be thankful to Him, and bless His name.*" If you are looking at the shambles of a life, you must ask yourself what thoughts you are allowing to stand and whether you are like the psalmist or the Israelites who died off in the wilderness. God's mind has no negatives; why should ours?

What You Feed Grows; What You Allow to Stand Increases

I am frequently heard telling my congregation, "What you feed grows, and what you starve dies." This is one of the most basic truths of our spiritual walk—if you feed good, godly things into your soul, your faith walk will grow. If you feed propaganda to your doubts and negativity, they will swell and consume your life like a cancer.

As often as I say that statement, there is another part I do not utter as often: "What you allow to stand increases, but what you pull up dies." Everyone who has ever gardened understands this—if you fail to pull the weeds, they will quickly grow up to choke out the good plants.

> **W**HAT YOU ALLOW TO STAND INCREASES, BUT WHAT YOU PULL UP DIES.

It is very difficult to never observe soul-polluting things in this life, and many people do not grow up in Christian homes and have received lots of negative seeds. The enemy's propaganda may have already been planted in you, but that does not mean you have to let those things *stand*. But if you feed your soul the pure milk of the Word, and uproot, tear down, destroy, and overthrow the works of the enemy, the things of God will increase in your life.

We cannot embrace both the enemy's propaganda and God's

promises and expect to prosper. James 4:8 says, "*Draw near to God and He will draw near to you. Cleanse your hands, you sinners; and purify your hearts, you double-minded.*" You can't be double-minded with God— you can't let ugly thoughts *and* beautiful thoughts stand. You can't meditate on negative thoughts and God's promises at the same time. You cannot allow sinful things to coexist with righteous things—you must *choose*. Which will you build up, and which will you tear out?

In heaven your thoughts speak even louder than words, which we will talk more about in chapter 15. You can calculate your words to impress or get the response you want, but your thoughts are the very essence of who you are and where your life is headed. And God knows the thoughts of your heart—even before you have them. This is why it is imperative that you take every thought captive and detoxify your soul.

How do we do this? Our church's Take Every Thought Captive media fast is one way we have sought to do it as a church. Every year, we shut down the flow of pollution and break the habits. It is important to take time to focus on God and His Word and to shut off the enemy's lies and deception.

This is one of the reasons God instituted feasts for the people of Israel—they served as joyful times and reminders of what God had done for them as a people. And were not to just remember the facts; they were to relive His majesty, as though He were doing for them what He had done for their ancestors. Every feast was also a rehearsal and preview of what Jesus would do for them.

They celebrated the feasts every year, different feasts at different times of the year, to draw their minds back to what God had done and what He was going to do. We must do the same, because we leak, and we forget what Jesus has done in our lives and the glory we will live out in eternity.

No Coexistence

I have seen that as human beings, we want it both ways—we want to be good when we want to be and do what we want the rest of the time. However, we fail to understand that the Holy Spirit's thoughts cannot coexist with unrighteous thoughts. When you try to do both, you will miss out on the best of His counsel and blessing because you allow unrighteous thoughts to stand.

> THE HOLY SPIRIT'S THOUGHTS CANNOT COEXIST WITH UNRIGHTEOUS THOUGHTS.

This does not mean that unrighteous thoughts will not come to you; they will. It just means that you must exercise your will to not allow them to stand and to ask for God's help to uproot them. You must be judging your thoughts, and the subjective standards of our culture are not the standard by which we judge them—only the standard of the Word of God is able to judge the thoughts of the heart.

Your thoughts, as we have said, determine the direction of your life—your way of life. You judge your thoughts, because your thoughts turn into your ways—your way of thinking, of acting, of conduct, of life. That is why Isaiah 55:8 says, "*'My thoughts are not your thoughts, nor are your ways My ways,' says the Lord.*" Thoughts and ways go together, and if you judge the first and let stand only that which is righteous, you will walk out ways that are right before God.

When my boys were young, we would take family vacations—road trips that were two weeks of turmoil. This was before DVD players or any other technology made keeping them busy easier, and they would be back there fighting and yelling at one another. We'd shout back at them, "Now, who are you making happy? Are you making Jesus happy, or the devil happy?"

It may sound overly simplistic, but this is the fundamental question we must be asking ourselves: Will the thoughts we let stand make the devil happy, or will they make Jesus happy? Righteous thoughts cannot coexist with unrighteous thoughts. You must choose whose thoughts you will let stand in your life, and in doing so, you choose which will increase in your life and thus the fruit you will reap.

Be Single-minded—and at Peace

The unfortunate truth is that the doctrine and ideology we teach in churches do not always turn into ways, and one simple reason for this is that we are only studying it on Sunday. We are not living it *daily*—we are just toying with the ideas for a few hours on Sunday morning. When we do this, we are being double-minded.

James 1:6-8 says that we are to *"ask in faith, with no doubting, for he who doubts is like a wave of the sea driven and tossed by the wind. For let not that man suppose that he will receive anything from the Lord; he is a double-minded man, unstable in all his ways."* When we are conflicted and of two minds, with divided loyalty between God and the world, we are unstable in all we do—and we *will* have conflict.

You see, conflict is caused by conflicting patterns of thought. Conflict is the opposite of peace, and if you lose your peace, you will lose your creativity.

Right before my father passed away, he was listening to a set of tapes. This was 1973, and I did not know the preacher, but in the last hours of his life, he was listening to something that was so important he did so again and again. The messages were by Kenneth Hagan Sr., and the first one was on Mark 11:23—*"For assuredly, I say to you, whoever says to this mountain, 'Be removed and be cast into the sea,' and does not doubt in his heart, but believes that those things he says will be done, he will have whatever he says."*

I listened to the second, and it was on Mark 11:23. And so was the next. And the sermon after that was—guess what? Mark 11:23. And as I listened to the same passage preached repeatedly, it began to dawn on me: I'm double-minded. I realized I needed to believe the Word of God—truly believe it—not just as a theory or a doctrine, but really *believe* it deep down in my soul. I knew that if I did, and didn't doubt, that as I believed it, I'd act on it.

When we do not divide between the devil's propaganda and God's promises, when we let both stand in our lives, we are being double-minded, and we will experience conflict. It is our *job* to take every thought captive, through the power of the Holy Spirit who raised Jesus from the dead, and bring those thoughts into captivity and the knowledge of Christ.

I have people ask me specific things, like is it all right if I watch this or do that. But it is not my job to determine for you what you should be putting into your soul, nor is it your spouse's or pastor's job. It is your responsibility to pray

> IT IS YOUR RESPONSIBILITY TO PRAY AND ASK GOD TO SEARCH YOU AND IDENTIFY THE POLLUTION IN YOUR SOUL

and ask God to search you and identify the pollution in your soul—and then to use your will, your mind, and your emotions to control what you allow to stand in your life and what you uproot.

Ephesians 5 tells us why: we are a bride being prepared for our Bridegroom, and He desires to wash us clean and present us to Himself without spot or wrinkle. Jesus gave up His life for us to make us holy and clean, washed by the cleansing of God's Word, and He did this to present us to Himself as a glorious Church without blemish. He desires us to be holy and without fault—without pollution of the soul.

Rid yourself of whatever holds you back and pulls you down. In doing so, you prepare yourself for an eternity together with the Bridegroom and for a life on earth that is directed by His ways and leaves a godly legacy for others to walk in. This is especially important as you realize that even a small moment in time can have a great impact on the rest of your life. As I will show you in the next chapter, a single moment can turn into a lifetime.

11
A MOMENT TURNS INTO A LIFETIME

We should be living a life of adventure with the Lord. Life with God is an adventure, because He has great plans for our lives—plans to prosper us and not to harm us. But they are not necessarily plans for our *pleasure*, and if you live simply for your pleasure, you will do only what you are pleased to do. Living this way will not stretch you or make you grow or mature, and mature Christians are those who are not just looking for that which benefits them. They are looking for that which benefits the entire Kingdom of God.

God desires to stretch you, challenge you, and increase you; He wants to make you more effective and make you more mature. That process is definitely an adventure!

> **G**OD DESIRES TO STRETCH YOU, CHALLENGE YOU, AND INCREASE YOU.

So how do we embrace this adventure of maturing in God's plan for our lives—lives that will leave a legacy for others to follow? Many teachers address people's need to give—to tithe and give offerings so that the Lord can unclench their fists in order to put His blessings in our hands. But I believe even before you mature by learning to give, you must mature by learning what to *receive*.

We Receive by the Spirit

When I was born, my father was a pastor of a very small church in Florida—so small we had no nursery. I came into the services he was teaching almost immediately, and my mother held me while my little spirit soaked up the Word of God before I even knew English. You might wonder how I could credit this experience for pouring the Word of God into my spirit even though I was just a newborn—how could I receive it?

Because our spirits pick up on more than our minds do.

Jesus and John the Baptist were still in the womb when Mary went to visit her cousin Elizabeth. Yet when Elizabeth heard the announcement that Mary was pregnant with the Savior, the babe within her womb leapt for joy. How could that happen? Baby John the Baptist did not speak Hebrew or Aramaic, but his *spirit* received more than his mind did.

Now this is not an argument against church nurseries. Instead, I desire that you begin to realize that what you allow into your life is of incredible importance. Your spirit can receive grace and life from God, or you can receive seeds of darkness and sin from the devil. Our spirits receive that which is spirit, and I want you to understand that *even a fraction of a moment is actually enough to influence your entire life.*

Changed In a Moment

Many of you reading this can remember the day when you were born again to new life through Jesus Christ. That moment changed your life forever, and you crossed a threshold of faith and into His glorious life.

You accepted His free gift of salvation and went from this world of darkness and into His wondrous light. Perhaps you can remember the day you were filled with the Holy Spirit and how He gave you utterance with other tongues. This changed your spiritual life forever.

Others have experienced God's healing, altering the course of their lives. Some of us have been delivered and set free from horrible bondages or afflictions or any number of other things—all in a moment of time after which we were never the same.

Moments in time can dramatically impact our lives, but some people's lives seem to have been influenced by good moments and others by bad moments. We all have both good and bad things happen to us, but I want to explore why some people experience bad moments but *do not let those things change them*. Why do some people seem to be going from glory to glory, while others suffer falls from seemingly ever-greater heights?

If we place our focus on the bad moments, our lives can go in the direction of hurt, anger, and fear. But if we focus on godly, liberating moments, it will take you on God's exciting adventure for your life.

Second Corinthians 3:18 says, *"But we all, with unveiled face, beholding as in a mirror the glory of the Lord, are being transformed into the same image from glory to glory, just as by the Spirit of the Lord."* We who have accepted Jesus should be transformed ever more to match His glorious image by seeing and reflecting God's glory. These are good moments that shape our lives.

When you learn to receive His glory, His glory is what will come out of you. You will reflect it on a dark and hurting world.

I believe that one of the keys to not allowing life's bad moments to capture our attention is fixing our eyes on God's glory. Keep your focus on Him. But the flip side to that is that we must in turn guard our hearts against those bad moments and the influence of destructive forces on our spirits.

Three Hundredths of a Second

Proverbs 4:23 (AMP) says, *"Keep and guard your heart with all vigilance and above all that you guard, for out of it flow the springs of life."* We can guard our finances against poor spending habits, watch our mouths so we don't speak the negative over our lives, and guard our relationships so they stay healthy, but Proverbs tells us that above all else, we must guard our own hearts.

When you fail to guard your heart, you can be infiltrated by darkness, fear, and sin because you have not put a watch over the health of your soul.

It takes only three hundredths of a second for our brains to establish a memory network from an outside stimulus. And it will begin and remain an established pattern of thinking and behavior that can influence the rest of our lives once it's formed.

Focusing on Jesus and the good in our lives is just one step—a foundation. But we must guard our hearts daily, for in the blink of an eye, in an unguarded moment, you can form a new pattern of thinking because of something you saw, heard, or experienced that you may have to deal with for the rest of your life.

The moment you accepted Christ, your world changed for the better. Now that you are saved and filled with His Holy Spirit, it is your full-time job to put a guard over your heart so that the devil cannot implant the seeds of your destruction.

Three hundredths of a second can change your entire perspective—for life. That's why, friend, you must be careful as a Christian. What you allow in can begin to formulate your life in a moment that turns into a lifetime.

The agenda of a lustful, greedy, and prideful society bombards us every day, and none of us are immune to it. If you have not purposed yourself to guard against this soul pollution and are not walking with the Spirit and the armor God has provided for you, the god of this world will seek to implant within you a seed of destruction to take your eyes off Christ and put them on the dark and dying things of his realm.

It seems like every day we hear of another minister or person of God who has been publicly found to be in private—or not so private—sin. But I guarantee that none of these fallen men and women woke up one morning and arbitrarily decided to have an affair or other moral failing. It happened slowly, in unguarded moments with the seed of one thought or impression at a time that took root and bore disastrous fruit.

You see, our adversary does not show you his long-term plans for your life, ending in your ruin and destruction. He comes one compromise at a time—one opportunity to let something in at an unguarded moment. It might be a pornographic spam email, or a scene in a movie, or a shady financial tip from a co-worker—opportunities to compromise on your convictions can come at any time.

Some time ago, a young woman who was in the Goth community began attending our church. She had many piercings, dressed all in black, and had numerous challenges. Tragically, she ended up taking her life. Other young people who dressed in that style who attended our church and who had been around her were shocked and awakened by her tragedy. They wondered, "Is this what lies in store for me? Is this what my path leads to?" They had never seen the end result of the dark path of pain and rejection the devil had started them on, but this poor girl's horrible tragedy opened their eyes to the devil's endgame.

> OUR ADVERSARY COMES ONE COMPROMISE AT A TIME.

We must guard our hearts and be mindful that the devil will not disclose his plans openly—but he will give you one moment at a time to compromise and let his influences into your life. When we see a prominent person or even friends and neighbors who fall, we must pray for them and see in their example the fruits of the devil's schemes.

Where did the path that saw a man's ministry destroyed by homosexual temptations begin? How did that happen? Where did that woman's path start that saw her leave her husband and children for another man? Where did that lifestyle of alcohol or substance abuse start? These things began one experience, one flirtation, and one glass at a time, but they all end in horribly damaged lives. They are all moments—moments in time where we can choose to guard our hearts or let evil in.

Shut the Door

I am always careful when I travel because roaches can get into your bags, and then you take them home with you. It is far easier to keep them out of your house than it is to get rid of them. The same is true of the destructive seeds the devil seeks to slip into your life one moment at a time. It is easier to keep them out than it is to deal with the damage they cause down the road.

If you want to prevent the bad things of life from gaining your focus, the best plan is to not let them into your heart in the first place! You must shut the door on the devil. This begins by accepting the fact that though the salvation you accepted—which changed your life in a moment—was free from the Lord, it also costs *everything*.

If you are in Christ, you are not your own—you were bought with a price. That price was high beyond compare: the death of Jesus Christ on the cross. Paul called himself a slave or bondservant of Christ, and he tells us, *"For you were bought at a price; therefore glorify God in your body and in your spirit, which are God's"* (1 Corinthians 6:20).

By no means do I say this to put guilt or condemnation or a burden on anyone. However, this is an important point because these moment-by-moment lures of the devil are always tied to selfish desires and pride. When we as mature believers forsake our selfish desires and seek first His kingdom, we do not give the devil space to work. The door stays shut. Guarding your heart because you are His and He paid the highest price imaginable for you is a different story than guarding your heart for your own sake.

Yet we all know that try as hard as we might, we are only human and we live in a fallen world. Bad things will happen; how we handle them is what counts. Let us look at some of the negative patterns of thought the devil tries to institute in our lives, because though the Holy Spirit may be shutting your door now, it may have been open since your early years.

12
GUARDING THE GATES OF YOUR SOUL

A check in your spirit is an inner sense that the Holy Spirit is trying to tell you something. It is a warning, like the check engine warning light in your car—a hesitancy or feeling of resistance about what you are doing. Before you take one more step, you must examine that "check spirit" light to see if God is trying to tell you something. The more you sensitize your spirit, the more you will become accustomed to receiving God's impressions straight from His Spirit to yours.

The patterns of thought the devil seeks to use to dominate your life come in one moment at a time—and remember, just a fraction of a moment, three hundredths of a second, can influence your entire life.

I have seen the devil trying to establish a pattern of anger in people. In a moment of time, you can lose your temper. And God forbid someone try to correct you then—that can make you even angrier! But the next time, it becomes a little easier to lose your temper, because you are establishing a pattern. Years later, you can really have an anger problem.

I see many people with codependency patterns. They have become so dependent on another person's opinion or acceptance that they are addicted to it. Instead of looking to the Lord for their sense of worth and approval, they have established a pattern of receiving it from another person—in ways that are often not very healthy. And each time that pattern is reinforced, it grows stronger. The same is true for the manipulative or strong-willed person that dominates or controls a weaker person—that sense of power they gain from manipulating the dependent person feels good to some part of them, and they repeat the pattern.

Fear can easily become a pattern—a moment in time can be indelibly etched in your mind from a terrifying experience. It can spill fear over into other areas of your life until you are motivated and directed not by God's will, but by fear.

Spending money can become a negative pattern. Perhaps, there was a time when you were not feeling so good about yourself, you bought something—and that began a habitual pattern of spending to make yourself feel better. Your bank account and credit card can't handle this type of treatment for your inner problems!

All these things and so many more can come into our lives if the door to our hearts is open just a crack. A crack is all the enemy needs, because he slips these things in a moment at a time.

Whom the Son Sets Free . . .

Many of these patterns can enter our lives when we are just children. Research shows many types of inappropriate sexual desires come from early childhood experiences—neurological patterns that begin early in our lives and are then reinforced in children who are helpless against abusers.

Whether you have patterns that you allowed in or that happened to you as a child, there is *hope*! One reason Jesus came was to set us free from these patterns. Listen to His passion as He describes His mission on earth: "*The Spirit of the Lord is upon Me, because He has anointed Me to preach the gospel to the poor; He has sent Me to heal the brokenhearted, to proclaim liberty to the captives and recovery of sight to the blind, to set at liberty those who are oppressed; to proclaim the acceptable year of the Lord*" (Luke 4:18-19).

He came to free you from the bondage of sin and death. In another place He says, "*Therefore if the Son makes you free, you shall be free indeed*" (John 8:36). You do not have to live with any bondage of hell upon your life—He has set you free!

When you operate in the freedom and liberty of walking in a righteous pattern before the Lord, that becomes a stimulus. It sets a new cycle; it sets a new pattern.

> **W**HETHER YOU HAVE PATTERNS THAT YOU ALLOWED IN OR THAT HAPPENED TO YOU AS A CHILD, THERE IS HOPE!

No matter how many patterns of behavior the devil has slipped through the crack of the door to your heart, Jesus can set you free. Those new in Christ frequently experience this freedom as a total paradigm shift. For those of us who have walked with Jesus for some time, however, we need God's grace to shut the door to the devil in our everyday lives and behaviors—and yet we do not always do so.

I would like to share with you why I think the devil can still find an opening to the doors of our hearts. It may very well be the greatest sin a believer can commit.

The Sin of Neglect

A certain farmer's fields yield an abundant harvest every year. He uses the best seed, and he irrigates the land throughout the long growing season. He tends the fields meticulously, tilling the earth, using the best fertilizers, and preventing weeds and bugs from getting into his crops through hard hours of difficult toil. His fields grow high and ripen under his watchful eye, and then the difficult labor of harvest begins—he spends many hours, rising very early and retiring very late.

This farmer grows older, and with no children who wish to take over the farm, eventually he sells it to retire. A younger man buys it for a good price, because the land has always been fertile and he expects a good return on his investment.

But this younger man doesn't see the value in spending money on pricey fertilizers and spraying for bugs. Keeping the irrigation channels repaired is hard work as well, and he has many other things that he wants to spend his time on.

When it is harvest time, he looks out at his fields and finds they do not look like they did when he bought them from the old farmer. The weeds have grown in with the crops, and the bugs have eaten their fill. Whole areas are brown and dead because they did not get enough water. What he does harvest is partly spoiled because he does not get it in fast enough and the rains come.

This young man may complain and question the wisdom of his purchase when he sees the return on his investment, wondering why the land has not blessed him as it did the old man from whom he bought it and why God liked the old man better. But it was not the land that did not bless this young man, nor was it that God loved the old farmer more.

The young man reaped what he sowed, for he cultivated a harvest of neglect in the once prosperous fields of a good steward.

We read about good stewardship throughout the Bible in many places, but one small verse from the apostle Paul stands out to me: "*It is required in stewards that one be found faithful*" (1 Corinthians 4:2).

Stewards must be faithful to that which is given to them. The field of our lives is not our own; it was bought with a price. And I believe that one of the greatest sins we can commit as Christians is in turn neglecting that which cost Christ everything.

We are stewards of our lives, and when we are not on guard—when we are lax in guarding our hearts and allow the devil to sow his seeds of darkness and sin—we are committing the sin of neglect. And the real trouble is that our enemy is not a passive foe. He is actively seeking our destruction, and our neglect gives him an opening.

> STEWARDS MUST BE FAITHFUL TO THAT WHICH IS GIVEN TO THEM.

Jesus tells this parable: "*The kingdom of heaven is like a man who sowed good seed in his field; but while men slept, his enemy came and sowed tares [weeds] among the wheat and went his way*" (Matthew 13:24-25). The enemy is the devil, and make no mistake—your enemy is seeking opportunities to seed the field of your life with the cares of this world and with sins that will destroy your life as well as rob you of your harvest or legacy.

We are all called to be good stewards, but make no mistake—your responsibility will be tested. Peter warns us, "*Be sober, be vigilant; because your adversary the devil walks about like a roaring lion, seeking whom he may devour*" (1 Peter 5:8).

The good news is this: if we stay in Christ, the enemy is a *toothless* lion. If we guard our hearts and are sober stewards of the new life God has given us through Christ Jesus, He gives us the power to shut the door on him. I would like to give you six practical thoughts on how to shut the door on the enemy and be more effective for the Kingdom of God.

Six Keys
Key 1: Keep Your Focus on God and His Word

The first key I'd like to share with you is one we have talked about before: Keep your focus on God. Another way to say this might be to keep a clear vision of the Word of God. God's Word will help you have a razor-sharp focus on His kingdom and not this sinful, earthly one. When your eyes are in the Word, your focus will be there too.

Stay focused on God's promises to you—they are infinitely better than the temptations for short term pleasure or gain the enemy offers you to crack the door open for him.

Key 2: Be Sensitive to the Holy Spirit

Another vitally important key is developing sensitivity to the presence of God and the moving of the Holy Spirit. The Word and the Spirit work together. You can think of it like this: the Word is the Sword of the Spirit, and the Holy Spirit shows you how specifically to use the Word you have put inside of you. If you have the Spirit without the Word, you are missing your sword in battle. Likewise, if you have the Word but no sensitivity to the Holy Spirit, you can miss how He is telling you to wield the Word as a weapon against the enemy.

Neglecting the Word can destroy you. You may think that you are the exception to the rule and that you can just operate by the Spirit, but we are easily deceived. Without the Word to keep you grounded you can get off into any number of crazy things. Neglecting the Word can destroy you, and neglecting the Holy Spirit will leave you dry and lacking direction.

Key 3: Cultivate Endurance

The Bible is filled with cautions about quitting when it gets tough. In Matthew 13 Jesus tells the Parable of the Sower. Some seed fell on rocky soil—the plants sprouted up but then withered away when it got hot. Don't let that describe the field of your life, because it *will* get hot!

Paul talks about having run the race set before him, and the writer of Hebrews says that we must "*let us lay aside every weight, and the sin which so easily ensnares us, and let us run with endurance the race that is set before us*" (Hebrews 12:1). This race is not a sprint; it's a marathon.

I cannot think of a more poignant statement about shutting the door on the devil and then staying true for the long haul than this admonition from Hebrews. Run the race with endurance.

Key 4: Know God Intimately

In the story of the prodigal son, we see that though the elder brother lived his whole life with this loving, compassionate father, he did not know his father's heart. I believe from this we can learn that you may know the Word, and you may even walk in signs and wonders, but if you do not intimately know the compassionate heartbeat of the Father, you are missing the point.

> IF YOU DO NOT INTIMATELY KNOW THE COMPASSIONATE HEARTBEAT OF THE FATHER, YOU ARE MISSING THE POINT.

A lot of people know Jesus only as Savior—they see Him as fire insurance against hell. But thinking of Jesus like that only would be like thinking of my wife as only a cook. If I thought of my wife only like that, I would be in trouble! And more than that, I would be missing out on the depth and giving nature of a loving and amazing woman.

Do not limit your intimacy with God and see Him one-dimensionally—become intimately acquainted with Him. Know Him not only as Savior but also as the Lord of your life—as the Healer, as the Provider, as your Peace. Know Him as your victory banner when you go into warfare against your enemy, the devil.

This will not happen in a casual relationship with God or if you take Him for granted. If you only pick up and dust off your Bible on Sunday to take it to church, you are missing the opportunity of a lifetime—intimately knowing the Lord of the universe and His plans for your life.

Key 5: Power Proofs

Perhaps you have heard the phrase "A tree is known by its fruit."

This is true of our lives. When we are stewarding our lives the way God intends, we will bear much fruit—and the fruit will be in signs, which I call power proofs.

Jesus told us, "*And these signs will follow those who believe: In My name they will cast out demons; they will speak with new tongues . . . they will lay hands on the sick, and they will recover*" (Mark 16:17,18). These things are the fruit of those who are stewarding their lives with sobriety, and we must be open to God using our lives to minister through powerful proofs that He is in us.

When someone in your home is sick, lay hands on that person and pray, *fully expecting* God to heal! When the devil is trying to push open the door and sow destruction in your life, cast him out! Head knowledge of the Word and the Spirit is not enough; we must activate this power in our lives by being open to what the Holy Spirit wants to do through us. This kind of fruit is not just for special Christians like preachers and people with television ministries—these signs follow *those who believe*. If you are a follower of Christ Jesus, that means *you*, friend.

Key 6: Leave No Room in Your Inn

If it only takes a moment for your brain to create a new neural pathway and your door is cracked open to the enemy, he can and will establish patterns in your life that lead to destruction. If, however, you are guarding the door to your heart, the events of life do not have to lead you downward, even if they are difficult.

The Word tells us that God works all things to our good for those who love Him and walk according to His purpose. So if you are inhabited by His thoughts, His heart, His Spirit, and His Word, you will leave no opportunity for the devil to get access to your heart—and there will be no room even if he tried. Those who are inhabited with God's presence will inhabit His kingdom.

In 2 Timothy 2:4 (NIV), Paul tell us, "*No one serving as a soldier gets entangled in civilian affairs, but rather tries to please his commanding officer."* The "civilian" life of this world is corrupt, and we are soldiers for the cause of Christ. We cannot let ourselves be distracted and caught up by the affairs of this world, for only Jesus has the keys to life. Our Commanding Officer, Christ Jesus, must dominate our focus.

> OUR COMMANDING OFFICER, CHRIST JESUS, MUST DOMINATE OUR FOCUS.

Be a Good Steward of God's Grace

Much of this chapter has focused on what we as believers can do to guard the door to our hearts, and I want to ensure that there is no misunderstanding. We have responsibility as good stewards of the fields of our lives, which the Lord bought and paid for. But I love God's grace.

Grace pours out over each of us when we come to Christ—a tidal wave of His blood that washes away every sin. We cannot earn it or do anything to merit it. Saul had not done a thing to be worthy of a visitation from Jesus on the Damascus road, but Jesus did visit him. But that does not mean it will be that way every time.

God's grace is a gift to us that we must not abuse, thinking that we can just go on sinning and trust in God's grace to come clean up our mess. We read in 1 Peter 4:10, *"As each one has received a gift, minister it to one another, as good stewards of the manifold grace of God."*

We must be good stewards of God's grace that sets us free and purpose within ourselves to shut the door of our hearts to the enemy. If you desire to be the kind of person who absorbs life's blows and still praises God, who does not have patterns in your life dominated by the devil, guard the door of your heart. Be a good steward over the gift He has given to you.

Life is an adventure with the Lord, and you can embrace God's maturing process for your life by guarding your heart and keeping your eyes on Jesus, giving no place to your enemy the devil. Let every moment of your lifetime be a sweet smelling sacrifice to the Lord, moments chained together to form a legacy for generations to come. Doing this is not easy—in fact, humanly it is impossible. That is why His Holy Spirit must guide us. Join me in the next chapter as I share how you can embrace being guided by eternity.

13

NO REGRETS

This is not a time to be casually sitting back and living life. In fact, you cannot live casually and expect to look back at your life and have no regrets. You must live it *strategically*. If you do not, your life will be consumed with regret. Regret is the cancer of life, and if you live your life casually, you will look back at the end and see that regret has eaten up your days.

> REGRET IS THE CANCER OF LIFE

Living strategically is especially important during seasons of great turmoil. New threats seem to be constantly arising, both at home and abroad. The world's economy is touchy—thank God that His economy isn't subject to debt crisis and foreclosure!—and sweeping political change has altered the political landscape of entire regions.

Everything that can shake is being shaken, and people are waking up to the fact that if they have not put their hope in something solid and secure, that hope is shaking and crumbling around them. Seasons of confusion and chaos are not when you want to try something new;

they are times for returning to the only proven truth to which man has ever grabbed ahold—God's Word.

The only way to strategically plan your life during periods of turmoil is by drawing your direction and goals from the Word of God. Some people think the Bible is just a philosophical book and that you can just take pieces and adopt them as good ideas for life. They think the Bible is just something to add to the teachings of the thinkers and philosophers of the day, creating a melting pot of concepts from which to cobble together a life.

But God's Word is not just a group of good ideas among many other equal voices. God's Word is the *only* truth, the only thing which is proven. Just the prophecies Jesus fulfilled as the Messiah are mind-boggling—the Old Testament is filled with literally hundreds of individual prophecies that Jesus fulfilled completely. The Bible's track record of accuracy is beyond any other book known to man.

We must grab hold of these truths and use them to govern lives that we have strategically aimed at the destiny God has for us. The alternative is to look back at lives consumed with regret and realize that instead of being aimed at the goal of God's destiny, we were instead driven to mediocrity.

What Drives You?

Some people do not realize that there is a world of difference between being a person with drive—a person living a strategic life aimed at goals—and being *driven*. When I get into my car, I decide where I want to go, and I drive. But if you are living your life casually instead of being guided by eternity, you will find that you are the one being driven. The question is, "What is driving you?"

The list is endless—work, wealth, possessions, recognition. However, it all boils down to this: driven people are most often gratified by accomplishment. They are driven to accomplishing something that is new and bigger than before. What they have attained is not enough—they feel the drive to always be pursuing that next great accomplishment in the hopes that it will satisfy this need, this drive within them that is not directed at the concrete truth of God's destiny.

Driven people are often preoccupied with the symbols of their accomplishments—nicer cars, bigger houses, and flashier toys. Is that new house a symbol of accomplishment? Yes, but it is also a symbol of debt for the next thirty years! All too often, we are preoccupied with the appearance of success, but when we are not letting God guide us, we are only grasping at shallow imitations of what true success should be.

When you are a driven person, you will find yourself caught up in an uncontrolled pursuit of expansion. But when is enough finally enough? How big a house do you need? How expensive must your car be? How much money do you need in the bank for enough to be enough? When you are driven, there is no good answer to these questions—you will find that you can never achieve enough to acquire peace.

That driving pursuit of more, more, more will often require cutting corners. That's why driven people have trouble with integrity. They might cheat on their tax returns or lie to get that deal at work—they will do what they think they can get by with if it means that they can get ahead.

Too often, driven people see "things" as the goal, and they are willing to sacrifice their integrity and their relationships with those around them in order to achieve what they think will give them peace and happiness. Their projects and desires are more important than people, and they are more oriented on achieving something temporary than on building relationships with other individuals, who are eternal. Often, they just use people instead of building lasting, meaningful relationships with them.

When you are driven, you simply don't have time. Driven people are abnormally busy, and they have no time for developing relationships or even being healthy, physically and emotionally. When you are too busy, it is easy to neglect what your body needs—proper rest, nutrition, and connections with others.

Emotional and physical lack of health often makes driven people angry—perhaps you know someone with a short fuse? Chances are good, this is a driven person. Oppose them, get in their way, or inconvenience them, and watch out—you'd better step back, because the over-driven person can explode!

So again I ask, "What drives you?" Or perhaps an even better question is, "Are you *driven*, or are you *driving*?" If the strategic aim of your life is to please God and follow His will and direction for your destiny, you will not be driven. You will have put Jesus in the driver's seat of your life, and side-by-side you can go where He directs.

> **A**RE YOU DRIVEN, OR ARE YOU DRIVING?

This image of moving together with Christ as the one directing your life makes me think of a wonderful Scripture in Matthew: "*Take My yoke upon you and learn from Me, for I am gentle and lowly in heart, and you will find rest for your souls. For My yoke is easy and My burden is light*" (Matthew 11:29-30). The image here is of two oxen yoked side by side to pull a heavy load—together. And let me tell you, He pulls far more than His own weight!

You will never find peace if you are driven. But if you follow the Lord's leading and walk beside Him, you find that Jesus guides you to rest for your soul and peace beyond your understanding.

God's Laws of Success

Deciding to face what drives you—and to instead put your life in order the way God desires—requires one simple (yet not too simple) thing: listening intently for the call of the Holy Spirit to guide you. Ceding your driven life over to God's destiny does not just happen because you want it to—you must cultivate a listening ear for the still, small voice with which the Holy Spirit speaks to us. You must listen for Him—and then obey.

The Holy Spirit speaks from the very nature of God. He says nothing apart from what the Father says, and when you tune out the things that drive you and listen to the Holy Spirit, you are listening to God's nature.

God blesses that which is in agreement with His nature. When you are listening to and obeying the Holy Spirit, God can bless your life in a way that surpasses human understanding.

If you are listening to prognosticators of doom and gloom on the news, supposed experts who write books, or even individuals who appear very successful because they are so driven, you will not be listening to the voice of the Holy Spirit for your guidance, correction,

> **G**OD BLESSES THAT WHICH IS IN AGREEMENT WITH **H**IS NATURE.

and wisdom. God cannot bless that which is opposed to His nature, so if you desire His blessing, you must learn and obey God's laws of success.

Law 1—The Law of Association

The people we spend time with are one of the single biggest influences on our lives. You have probably heard the saying, "Show me your friends, and I will show you your future." We call it peer pressure, but it goes beyond that. Modeling is the process where we learn from watching others. We surround ourselves with others, and we cannot help but hear how they speak, watch the way they do things, see how they dress, and even notice what interests them. And it all affects you.

David certainly understood this when he wrote, *"Blessed is the man who walks not in the counsel of the ungodly, nor stands in the path of sinners, nor sits in the seat of the scornful; but his delight is in the law of the LORD, and in His law he meditates day and night"* (Psalms 1:1-2).

The psalmist so clearly spells out the power of those who influence us—and the blessings that come from having a life guided by eternity and not by the negative influences around you. It is vitally important for you to build associations with godly people. The alternative is going down a dead-end path. I challenge you to read the rest of that psalm to see the blessings for the one who delights in the Lord as opposed to the ungodly.

You will gravitate toward the interests of those around you. Spend enough time around them, and it *will* happen. The people you associate with impart things to you such as information—it is just a question of whether it is a godly influence or not.

Attitudes can easily rub off on us from others. If you are around nice, wonderful people, it is easier to have a good attitude yourself. If those around you are angry, critical, or negative, that can rub off too. But the Bible tells us clearly that we are to think on whatever is true, noble, just, pure, lovely, and of good report—anything of virtue or that is praiseworthy (Philippians 4:8). If these are not the things those around you think and talk about, it might be time to change your associations.

I have found that people often have either an earthly wisdom or a godly wisdom. Earthly wisdom may sound good, but we know from the Word that God has chosen the foolish things of this world to put to shame the wise. Earthly wisdom may look good, but to God, it is foolishness—and the opposite is equally true.

> EARTHLY WISDOM MAY LOOK GOOD, BUT TO GOD, IT IS FOOLISHNESS

Even subtler than the type of wisdom people have is that those we associate with possess a kind of resource—everyone you are in touch with extends to you a new level of resource. They may know people or how to do things, or they may have advice, again potentially good or bad. They may have access to information, and it can be tempting to turn to them to solve our problems when we should be turning to God. God may choose to meet a need we have with the resources of those around us, but it is important to go to Him first and let Him direct our paths to the people He has in mind. Be careful of the resources you accept from those around you.

It may be controversial and easy for some to dismiss, but I am confident that because of the Law of Association, we also pick up on the spirit of those around us. Perhaps you have spent time with someone who is not living for the Lord only to find yourself plagued by lustful or inappropriate thoughts. Is that you? Are you prone to those tendencies? Or did you pick up on the spirit of that person? Bitterness, anger, or any other negative spirit work the same way—you must be cautious.

The only answer is to surround yourself with the Holy Spirit and His influences—and people who want God in their lives and who are pursuing the gifts of His Holy Spirit. How much better to focus on the glory and beauty and awesomeness of God, His incomprehensible love, and the magnitude of who He is than the spirits of this world! *That* is the Spirit I want to catch hold of!

The last element of the Law of Association that I want to cover is the impact that other people's vision has on us. The Word tells us that without a vision, we perish. Without a vision, you are lost. And if you are lost, then you do not know where you are going or what direction to walk in. Being lost and visionless like this, simply ambling through life, is a sure way to seed regrets in your life that will consume you. When you lack vision and a purpose, you are in a sense perishing.

But your vision must come from the right source, and when it simply comes from those around you, the vision you take on from these associations may not be the one God has intended for you. If their vision is locked on materialism and the things of this world, on always seeking that next accomplishment, or on the praise of men, it is a vision you do not want, and you must be careful.

God does not want you to waste your life visionless and without direction. He wants you to take your vision, your goals, and your dreams directly from His Spirit—not the spirit of another. The Law of Association says that you will take on the attributes of those you spend time with, and so it is clear that if you wish to take on the attributes of God and grasp His vision and direction for your life, you must spend time with Him—especially His Holy Spirit and His written Word. These are the ways in which we use this Law of Association to make us more like our Father and not like the people with whom we associate.

The Law of Association has a powerful impact on our lives, and we must determine whether we will be guided by eternity by spending time with God or if we will lose sight of His plan by taking on the likeness of people not modeling our Lord and Savior.

Law 2—The Law of Environment

Much like the Law of Association, where we spend our time—the Law of Environment—has a great deal of influence on us. *Your environment is the incubation chamber that will birth the outcomes of your life.* You must decide carefully what you will surround yourself with.

The womb is the best example of an incubating environment—we all started here in the perfect environment for growing and developing into a child who was mature enough to enter the world. Within our mothers' wombs were all the necessary materials to develop our lives, and the outcome—our births—was the predictable result of having spent the necessary time in the right environment.

What you surround yourself with now will determine the outcome of your life. Do you want your life to birth godliness, peace, and the closeness with the Spirit that results in a purposeful life? Then choose what goes into your environment wisely.

You can test some of the elements of your environment by asking God to examine your heart as you consider them. Are you more likely to miss church, or to miss your favorite show on TV? Do you choose to read the Word or *The Financial Times*? Where is your priority? Look at the godly elements in your life and those of this world, and ask yourself in all honesty which has your focus and priority.

Your environment is the incubation chamber that determines the future results in your life, so if you desire financial success, entertainment, or the gratification of your body, by all means choose the things of this world. But if you want God to birth in you firm direction, unshakable vision, strong leadership, and an enduring legacy, you must purposefully create an environment oriented on the things of God.

You have the power to choose your influences. To some this might seem like common sense, and others might read that and, seeing themselves as victims, argue, "I can't help it that my life is like this!" My wife is a great example of this. She was reared in a very hedonistic home—but she chose a different path. She heard about a church and went to it, where she heard the Word of God and met a wonderful Sunday school teacher, Shirley Mencer. She chose her influences, and because she did so, God birthed in her life many wonderful things and remarkable closeness to Him. Had she simply longed for change but stayed in the environment she was in, this would not have happened and she wouldn't be the amazing woman she is today.

> **YOU HAVE THE POWER TO CHOOSE YOUR INFLUENCES.**

God puts it so clearly in Deuteronomy 30:19 (NLT), which says, *"Today I have given you the choice between life and death, between blessings and curses. Now I call on heaven and earth to witness the choice you make. Oh, that you would choose life, so that you and your descendants might live!"*

If you wish to leave a lasting legacy by living a life guided by God, you must choose the right environment. You possess the power to choose a godly environment, which will incubate godly things in your life. Or you can choose to marinate in the things of this world, and all that you do and leave behind will be consumed in fire as wood, hay, and stubble.

In the next chapter, I want to show you two more of God's laws of success, as well as the senses a leader must cultivate. Choosing the right associates and environment is vital, but so too is understanding the power of focus and the nature of righteousness. Let us look at these together in the next chapter.

14

FOCUS, RIGHTEOUSNESS AND THE SENSES OF A LEADER

Your life is going to look like those you surround yourself with and the context of your environment. But let's also consider two more of God's laws—the Law of Focus, and the Law of Righteousness. First, let us talk about the power of focus.

Law 3—The Law of Focus

James 1:8 says it very plainly: "*A double-minded man* [is] *unstable in all his ways.*" Another version says these double-minded people, whose loyalty wavers, have loyalty that is divided between the world and God.

We have talked about the importance of the people with whom we associate and the environment with which we surround ourselves, but we have not talked about ourselves. It is vital that we fix our eyes on Jesus and that our faith and loyalty is in Him alone.

To me the best modern-day examples of people who are double-minded and unstable are to be found in politics. We call it the "flip-flop." A politician says one thing in one circumstance but for whatever reason may say something else—even the opposite—in another circumstance. Will we ever find a perfect leader? No, but we should select those with enough integrity to stand on the right side of an issue and not be swayed by fickle public opinion.

We must demand the same of ourselves. We must seek to be people of such integrity that we choose God's side of any issue and stick to it with both love and conviction.

I believe there are three elements to mastering the Law of Focus and letting it help make us people guided by eternity. The first is that your focus must be purpose-driven. So what is the purpose, and to whom should you look to learn it? While we all may have different visions, we are united in Christ by having a single mandate and focus: "*Seek first the Kingdom of God and His righteousness*" (Matthew 6:33).

> **YOUR FOCUS MUST BE PURPOSE-DRIVEN.**

You are not here for your kingdom. You are not here to expand your estate. You are here for the Kingdom of God. If you keep this in proper perspective, everything else will fall into proper order. The rest of that verse says, "*. . . and all these things shall be added to you.*" When your focus is driven by His purpose, you do not need to worry about the rest.

The next element of the Law of Focus is that *we must be principle-based*. What principles? Those in the Word of God. If your principles are changing along with the culture, you are not drawing them from the timeless Word of God, which is the only concrete truth known to man. If someone can negotiate you out of your principles, you are not living as a person of integrity.

We do not choose what is right and wrong, for when we choose to follow our own whims or those of the people around us, we are guided by earthly lusts and desires. The outcome will be a life consumed with regrets and crippled by sin. God's principles are timeless, and when we focus on them, we begin to reflect back His light for the whole world to see.

Finally, the last element of focus is that your focus must be bigger than yourself. It is not about us; it is about Him. It is about His kingdom and His principles, and we are choice heirs and inheritors of a promise that is so much bigger than any of us.

To please God, we must move in faith. Our focus must be on Him, trusting that He will put in our lives any good thing that is part of our destiny. If you are focused only on yourself, creating what you have the ability to create and doing what you have the power to do, you are giving God no glory. But if you walk in faith, He will call you to create things bigger than yourself and to do things more difficult than you can manage—and in those impossible situations, God shows up as mighty and able and glorious. When your focus is on expanding His glory on the earth, the end results will be far greater than you could ever dream of by yourself and will give glory to God. *That* is the power of the Law of Focus.

Law 4—The Law of Righteousness

The Law of Righteousness is quite simple: Righteousness is the only nature God can bless. Earlier we said that God blesses that which is in agreement with His nature, and God is righteous.

Now, do not be confused: our self-made righteousness is as filthy rags (see Isaiah 64:6). However, 1 John 3:7 says, "*Little children, let no*

> RIGHTEOUSNESS IS THE ONLY NATURE GOD CAN BLESS.

one deceive you. He who practices righteousness is righteous, just as He is righteous." When we obey God and do what is right, it shows that we are righteous, even as Christ (who made us right with God) is righteous. When what we do lines up with the Word of God, He can bless it.

When a nation does what is righteous in God's sight, no matter its background, God can bless it (at least to a certain degree). The United States of America is like this—it was founded on the principles of God's Word. And He has blessed it! The Bible says that righteousness exalts a nation—but watch out as our country steers farther and farther from God's truth and toward sin and moral relativism. Will He continue to bless our country? For all our sakes, I pray that godly people who will lead us into paths of righteousness will be elected to lead this country.

Righteousness exalts a nation, but it also lifts up a family, or even an individual. So if you do not feel lifted up, I suggest you look at whether or not you are living righteously.

Many people have come to me who are not being lifted up, wondering why God wasn't blessing them. These people often have it all together on the outside, but I have found that there can be a secret sore festering: their thought life.

When God is not exalting us, we must carefully examine what thoughts we entertain. The word "entertain" combines "enter" and "retain"—so I ask, *"What thoughts that come in are you allowing to stay?"* Unrighteous thoughts can come to all of us, even those who have walked with Christ for a long time. The enemy will always tempt, but we do not have to give in to the temptation—not just in what we actually *do*, but whether or not we dwell on the thoughts and temptations he suggests.

This is why it is so vital to be guided by eternity and listening closely to the Holy Spirit. The devil will seductively suggest a temptation to you, and while your sinful nature may cry loudly for you to entertain that thought, the Holy Spirit's voice is a gentle whisper you must train yourself to hear. If you hear the Holy Spirit speaking and you entertain *His* thought, then God can bless your life. But if you entertain temptation even just in your private thought life, you will not be walking in the righteousness that God can bless.

Our hearts should cry out with the psalmist, who wrote, "*Let the words of my mouth and the meditation of my heart be acceptable in Your sight, O LORD, my strength and my Redeemer*" (Psalms 19:14).

We can all be tempted to compromise on our righteousness. But noble men and women decide *in advance* to take compromise off the table when it comes to their convictions—righteousness is choosing God's way and sticking with it, no matter the perceived benefits. No benefit of the moment outweighs the blessing of God.

Willpower alone will not let you live a righteous life. Left on our own, we ultimately lack the strength. That is why we so badly need the Holy Spirit in our lives, telling us how to handle situations and being that strength within us that we need to say no to temptation and to live by our godly convictions instead of what is convenient. I have found that conviction and convenience cannot work well together. You must choose one or the other—and God only blesses one.

The moment you stop being led by your honor, you start faking greatness. The moment you leave behind conviction and righteousness for what seems best in the moment, is the moment you cease shaping a godly legacy for others to follow.

> **T**HE MOMENT YOU STOP BEING LED BY YOUR HONOR, YOU START FAKING GREATNESS.

The temptation to compromise on righteousness will only grow stronger, and the separation between light and darkness will only grow sharper. But it will only get brighter and brighter for those who walk in faith. Proverbs 4:18 is a seminal Scripture for me: "*But the path of the just is like the shining sun, that shines ever brighter unto the perfect day.*"

It is important to realize that true righteousness is not about knowing how to act the part and what words to say to come off like a godly Christian. The only testimony with your lips that matters is that which you back up with your life. And the only way to live out what God calls us to is by relying on Him and the work of His Holy Spirit to work out righteousness within us.

In my church, I speak on tithing and giving. It is not that I want or need the congregants' money; instead, I want them to know God's blessings when they obey His principles. Yet even after years of walking this out in my life and preaching it from a pulpit, I still must actively choose righteousness in my life.

I was recently with one of my grandsons outside a grocery store when a woman stopped us on our way out. "Do you have two dollars?" she asked. "I live on the west side, and I have no way to get home."

My first reaction was to wonder if she would really spend the money on the bus. Or would she use it to buy alcohol or drugs? But very quickly I listened for the Holy Spirit, and I feel like I heard the Lord say, "This is okay."

"Dear lady, I don't have two dollars," I told her. "I only have five." So I handed her a five-dollar bill and said, "May God bless you."

I do not know what she used that money for, but I know that I showed her with my life that I am a believer in Jesus and that I walk out the righteousness and principles I profess with my mouth. This was a small example, but that is how the Law of Righteousness plays out in our lives—through the little, daily things on which it is easy to compromise. Don't ever negotiate on the principles of righteousness, and God will bless your life.

The Five Senses of a Leader

I have told you about God's laws of success and how important they are for living a life guided by eternity and His Holy Spirit. Those are principles that any and every Christian should pursue in their lives. But as the darkness gets darker, the light must get brighter, and if you wish to leave a legacy behind, simply being like "any other Christian" is not enough. If you wish to be someone who leaves a legacy for the ages, you must be a *leader*.

Most people know we have five senses—hearing, sight, touch, smell, and taste. But just as there are godly laws for success, true leaders have five senses that have nothing to do with this crude physical world. Let us look at them together.

1. Sense of Debt

Debt is a word with many negative connotations, but leaders live with a sense of debt—it is the opposite of the attitude of entitlement. We must cultivate an understanding that we have not one good thing that has not come from God. We are indebted to the Lord. He has given you your life and salvation—in fact, even your next breath comes from Him as a gift.

We *deserve* none of it, but He has given us all of it—every blessing comes from Him. If you walk in thankfulness and have a sense of debt and gratitude for what He has given you, you are actively developing a leadership quality that is essential for being a godly leader and for leaving a legacy.

2. Sense of Devotion

Devotion is a word we seldom use these days, perhaps because profound dedication and loyal commitment to a person or cause is rare in our society. But a leader's devotion to Christ Jesus compels us to follow Him and obey His commands. One of the Holy Spirit's works is compelling us toward devotion to God.

A leader recognizes that it is not about his works and his kingdom—it is about the work of God and His kingdom! He died for us, and we were buried with Him, so it is not we who live but Christ who lives in us. If that is really true, we must cultivate a sense of devotion and dedication to the things that touch His heart and toward what compelled Jesus to endure the cross. He so loved the world that He gave Himself for it, and our sense of devotion must lead us to do the same that we might bring glory to His name and bring the lost to salvation.

> ONE OF THE HOLY SPIRIT'S WORKS IS COMPELLING US TOWARD DEVOTION TO GOD.

3. Sense of Direction

Often when you are lost, it is because you have lost your sense of direction. Godly leaders look to the Holy Spirit for a heavenly vision to gain a sense of *eternal direction*. They pursue God for a heavenly vision, a calling from God.

One of the chief things I pray when I dedicate little children to the Lord is that nothing would keep them from the destiny that God has for them—that they would find the direction and vision God has for them and not depart from it.

If you feel like you are living a careless, directionless life or that life's forces are driving you rather than you driving your life, you must stop and ask God for directions.

4. Sense of Destiny

Really this whole chapter comes down to the fact that leaders must have a sense of eternal destiny. They must live in the light of eternity. I do not just mean a sense of destiny as it pertains to what we do here on this earth; I mean that godly leaders

> LEADERS MUST HAVE A SENSE OF ETERNAL DESTINY.

must have a sense of *ultimate* destiny.

Everything in this world will one day come to an end. And since everything around us is going to be destroyed, what holy lives should we live—oriented not on this passing time on earth but on the eternal things God deems really matters!

5. Sense of Duty

I believe the concept of a leader's Christian duty has taken on a negative connotation in some circles as being too legalistic or too rigid. Just as surely as people lay down their lives for our country because of duty, true leaders must be prepared to lay down their own lives for the cross of Christ.

Paul expresses his sense of duty as a bondservant of Christ when he said he could take no credit for the lives changed by his ministry: *"For if I preach the gospel, I have nothing to boast of, for necessity is laid upon me; yes, woe is me if I do not preach the gospel!"* (1 Corinthians 9:16).

Our faith must compel us to act on the duty that one and all Christians possess: the commission Jesus gave us when He ascended to heaven. He told us all, *"All authority has been given to Me in heaven and on earth. Go therefore and make disciples of all the nations, baptizing them in the name of the Father and of the Son and of the Holy Spirit, teaching them to observe all things that I have commanded you; and lo, I am with you always, even to the end of the age"* (Matthew 28:18-20).

You might say that some are called to be evangelists and others are not. You might say that your leadership gifts run along a different course. But I tell you that while you may not lead from a pulpit, we all have a duty to witness. We have a duty to tell people about Jesus and make disciples of them!

But before you grow concerned over how you will do this, be sure you pay attention to what Jesus says near the end of the above quote: He is with us always. You do not witness alone—the Spirit bears witness with you! God sent the Holy Spirit, and He is the One who will show you what to say.

Having ambitions to be a leader and leave a legacy is common to many men and women. But you must realize that if you wish to leave a godly legacy, you cannot ignore God's rules of success or the five senses that God asks His leaders to possess. When you put all of this together, you will realize that you are keeping a perspective of eternal values at the forefront of your life. You are being guided by eternity.

15

SETTING YOUR AFFECTIONS

No matter how long you have been saved, it is important to periodically perform a self-inspection and re-evaluate your spiritual condition. David famously said, "*Search me, O God, and know my heart; try me, and know my anxieties; and see if there is any wicked way in me*" (Psalms 139:23, 24). We can all become very comfortable with our routine or with the moves that God has done in the past—but we must instead stay closely attuned to God and His goals for our lasting legacy.

If you do not want to miss what God may wish to do in the future, be sure you do not become mired in the past. There is nothing more important than being in the perfect will of God.

The Lord has spoken to me very clearly about one element in particular that is important for Christians to

> IF YOU DO NOT WANT TO MISS WHAT GOD MAY WISH TO DO IN THE FUTURE, BE SURE YOU DO NOT BECOME MIRED IN THE PAST.

examine frequently: where we set our affections. Some people have erroneously believed that what calls to them—what appeals to them in their hearts—is outside of their control. People can try to use this as an excuse to justify temptation, but the Lord desires that His people learn that *we*, not any outside force, have control over where we set our affections.

This is a very important area to frequently examine in your life, for if the desires of your heart are fixated on the carnal, material things of this world or things that are outright opposite God's will, your heart will not have the tender malleability He wishes it to have. He will not be able to guide it as He wills; it will be hard and preoccupied when He desires it to be sensitive and attuned to Him.

Staying on the right track as a Christian has a great deal to do with where you set your affections. The Word bears this out—and it also shows that it is in large part our responsibility as the Lord's servants to set our affections on that which is in agreement with His will.

You Set Your Affections

Whatever form of ministry you have in your life, where you set your affections determines a great deal about what God can do through you. And the Scripture is actually very specific about this: *you have the power to set your affections.*

Colossians 3:2 says, "*Set your mind on things above, not on things on the earth.*" You will want what you focus on, so if you are setting your focus on the things of God, that will be where your affections are.

Understand something: if you find your thoughts dominated by the things down here—nice cars, houses, vacations, achievements, accolades—you are setting your affections on things that are passing and temporary. God is not going to force your thoughts to come up to His level; what you set your affections on is a choice of your own will. You chose what you focus on, and what you focus on will drive your affections.

I once heard someone taking defensive driving school say that the instructor told him not to let his eyes be distracted by things off the road because it is your inherent tendency to go toward that which you focus on. You cannot continually look at things that are of this world and expect to somehow miraculously arrive at God's supernatural destination. If you desire to go where He wishes you to go, you must put your focus on Him—the things above, not the things below.

Setting your affections is your responsibility, and you do so through the empowerment of His Holy Spirit within you. This is obviously important so that in the end your destination leaves the lasting godly legacy that He intends for your life, but it is also very important for the simple day-to-day living and testimony you are to be. Because your affections do not simply determine your outcome; they also control your emotions.

Your Affections Control Your Emotions

Your affections will control your emotions, and what controls your emotions controls your life. This is absolutely fact. If you do not believe it, just watch when someone messes with something or someone you are deeply affectionate about—it will stir you emotionally! A mother bear is most ferocious when protecting her cub, and you can see in the most mild-mannered mother that a ferocious "mother bear" can suddenly emerge if someone threatens her children.

> YOUR AFFECTIONS WILL CONTROL YOUR EMOTIONS, AND WHAT CONTROLS YOUR EMOTIONS CONTROLS YOUR LIFE.

Your affections control your emotions—you are passionate about what you love. We can simply observe this in others and ourselves. But the interesting thing is that since you have the ability to set your affections, you can also then influence your emotions.

Some people say that they are unable to control their emotions.

They like to say that emotions are valid simply because they exist. And while I will not debate that you may have an emotion, and the fact that you have it means it is "real," that does not mean that they are all godly or legitimate. If you have set your focus on consuming, your affections will be on the material things of this world—and if you do not get them, they are threatened or lost, or someone messes with them, you will have an emotional reaction that may not be at all godly. You may feel greed, lust, covetous, envious, or any number of other emotions.

And just because you may experience these emotions as a Christian does not mean that you *should be* experiencing them—these emotions are evidence that your affections may be in the wrong place.

The world of advertising has perfected manipulating our emotions to an art form, because they know how to get people to set their focus on these primal, base emotions of desire. The commercials and ads you see are not designed to appeal to your rational mind; they are designed to appeal to your emotions by getting you to set your affection on the things they are advertising.

So you must decide whether or not you want the advertising agencies and Madison Avenue determining your affections—or if you want God to be the center of your focus.

Recalibrate Your Affections

We have to be careful what we focus on, because it will be consuming. That's why we are to behold the Lord and to set our affections on the things that are above, not below. *This*, my friend, is why we are told to pray without ceasing. That is why we must seek to spend time in His presence every day—to wrest our focus away from the things of this world and set them on the things above.

Interestingly, the biblical standard for dwelling in the presence of God is actually going before Him at least three times a day. We are to shut everything else out to be in His presence and focus on Him. Daniel did so while in Babylon, and it got him in trouble with the king's advisors. He did it so regularly it was the only thing they knew they could use to entrap him. Early morning, mid-morning, and evening, he went before the Lord to keep his focus on God.

Some people may take this and make it legalistic, but for me, it is not at all a thing of rigid structure or religion. I know I need my focus recalibrated—frequently! I know I need to "pray without ceasing" and make appointments with God. That is the key—it is not about routine, legalism, and dead religion.

Without being intentional about meeting Him, you will miss an appointment with God that He would like to use to recalibrate your focus and set your affections onto Him and the things of His kingdom.

Live from Heaven's Perspective

We live in a natural world—a physical world we can see and taste and touch. We perceive in three dimensions, but God is not limited to our understanding of the physical world. According to Einstein, there are at least four dimensions—minimum. Jewish rabbis say there are eleven, and while we may never know how many there are, God exists in all of them and perceives all of them. God's dimension is a spiritual one we may not be able to see with our eyes but is completely real nonetheless, and we must learn to live from the dimension of God's perspective.

WE MUST LEARN TO LIVE FROM THE DIMENSION OF GOD'S PERSPECTIVE.

We train our emotions and attention to focus on the natural world from birth. Our affections get set on natural things and natural happenings, but when we are born again, we must ask the Holy Spirit to open our eyes to the unseen world so that we can learn to live from heaven's perspective.

Paul prayed that God would give the Ephesians *"the spirit of wisdom and revelation in the knowledge of Him, the eyes of your understanding being enlightened; that you may know what is the hope of His calling, what are the riches of the glory of His inheritance in the saints, and what is the exceeding greatness of His power toward us who believe, according to the working of His mighty power"* (Ephesians 1:17-19). Yet all too often Christians live as though this physical world is all there is, and their eyes are not enlightened to the riches of God's glory.

A few years ago I was in Ghana, Africa, preaching at a church God has used to touch literally millions of lives. Someone got up and announced during one of the meetings that one of their pastoral staff had just died, and I was utterly amazed at the response of the pastors sitting around me.

Instead of mourning the passing of one of their fellow pastors, these men of God were elated—they counted him so fortunate and blessed that he had headed to his true home and was now with Christ. They lived as though heaven was more real and more desirable than the world we live in. Paul understood this so well and wrote, *"For to me, living means living for Christ, and dying is even better . . . I'm torn between two desires: I long to go and be with Christ, which would be far better for me. But for your sakes, it is better that I continue to live"* (Philippians 1:21,23-24 NLT).

The truth is that heaven, the spiritual world, is more real—and more permanent—than this temporary "real" world we live in daily. The more we can live with our affections guided by a heavenly perspective, the more we will bring God's perspective into this physical world we inhabit and leave His imprint on our legacy.

You *Are* the Message

Because of our potential for bringing God's perspective into our natural lives, we have an opportunity to not simply spread His message. We do not just *have* a message, we *are* a message! Every word and action reveals who you are. Every day, I'm revealing to my children and my children's children, my spiritual children, my friends, my associates, my *oikos*. *Oikos* is a word from the Greek that means all our relationships and acquaintances. We live a message every day.

The Lord just didn't send words, He sent *the* Word. The Word became flesh and dwelled among us, and we beheld Him as the only begotten Son of God, full of grace and truth. It's not enough to preach, we must *live*. You are a message.

You are God's narrative truth on the earth, and what you do, how you live, what you say, what you respond to, what you hold dear, and what you strive to accomplish are all God speaking a story through your life. Stop and let that sink in—how would really living with that understanding impact how you operate daily?

We are to preach and live out the eternal truth of God's Word, giving it to humanity with our very lives.

We began this chapter asking God to examine our lives, and when you consider that you are a living message, that becomes even more important. It is interesting how aspects of our natural lives can show us our spiritual condition.

Consider how you respond under pressure, because how you respond when pressed exposes the *real you*. We have all failed in this area, but we should be glad pressure exposes what is really inside, because then we know what to work on with God. Besides, how you even recover from messing up when pressed is a message in itself.

So we have talked about the importance of setting your affections, but in the next chapter I want to talk not about your affections but your *mission*. Your life is a message, but you also have a mission. Would you like to know what it is?

16
EMBRACE YOUR LIFE'S MISSION

It is not enough to just know you are a message—you must give your life a *mission* if you truly wish to be complete as a person. Simply living a message is a wonderful start, and God's message to the world is the most important news we could ever bear. But within that message God has a purpose for you that you must embrace if you want to feel the kind of fulfillment only God can give you.

YOU MUST GIVE YOUR LIFE A MISSION IF YOU TRULY WISH TO BE COMPLETE.

I have heard that one of the difficult things about being incarcerated is that if you have nothing to do, nothing to accomplish, nothing to give, and nothing to create, it deprives you of a sense of purpose that all human beings crave at some level. They tell me solitary confinement is the worst punishment you can ever have because you can't create—you have no mission, you have no purpose. Because of this, you have no worth and you have no self-esteem.

If a loss of mission and purpose is so devastating to those deprived of it, should we not strive to use our freedom to discover and live out God's purpose for our lives with everything in us?

A message with no mission accomplishes nothing. What are you accomplishing? What are you focusing on? Where are your affections?

Some of us are called into ministry—to touch the lives of congregations, or youth, or the unsaved. Others are missionaries, called to take the gospel to specific people groups or areas of the world. But far more people are not "in the ministry." Yet simply living a message is not enough—we can all learn God's purpose for our lives and then live out that mission on the earth.

I like the saying, "Small can reach where big cannot"—you can minister to lives you touch daily in ways that the most powerful televised ministry cannot do. Your life is a message, but you can live out your mission daily and with people who may never encounter someone in full-time ministry. Every message needs a mission.

When we started our church, God gave me several principles. One of the most important was that in every sermon I preached, He wanted me pointing people to a vision or message. I have preached vision since our fist service. When I spoke the vision God had given me for the church and what it would be like, I told them what we would accomplish for world missions—giving millions towards spreading the gospel. And we have seen it come to pass because God used that sense of vision to unite the congregation and promote spreading the gospel.

The Word says, "*Where there is no vision, the people perish*," (Proverbs 29:18 KJV). Without a mission, you will live a life of constant wandering. You will go here and there and try this and that, seeking the fulfillment God would give you in accomplishing His purpose for you on the earth. Do not be like the Children of Israel who wandered in the wilderness for forty years on a journey that should have taken less than forty days—embrace God's mission for your life.

Wise Up

If you want to live a life that is fulfilled and complete, you must live the mission God has for your life. But one of the most common questions I'm asked is, "How do I learn what that mission is?" I can give you the answer in one word: *wisdom*.

Wisdom is essential in the pursuit of fulfillment. "*Wisdom is the principal thing; therefore get wisdom. And in all your getting, get understanding,*" the writer of Proverbs tells us (Proverbs 4:7). Getting wisdom is the wisest thing you can do! And whatever else you do, develop good judgment.

We talked about the importance of setting your affections, but wisdom is the single most important element in *how* we go about setting our affections and defining our mission. In fact, it should be the first affection on which you set your focus—first set your affections on gaining wisdom and understanding!

I love the Lord's presence. I would rather be dead than to not have His presence in my life, but His presence has drawn me toward the pursuit of wisdom. In my opinion, the pursuit of wisdom is the foremost act of worship that a person can live.

I love worshiping the Lord and the impact that has on a life. I love seeing His miracles and His dramatic moves on the earth. But the Children of Israel give us an excellent example of what can happen when we lack wisdom. God's presence was so strong that He literally *split the Red Sea*, but because they lacked wisdom, the Children of Israel wandered the wilderness for forty years. You can praise, you can see miracles, and you can experience other moves of God, but if you are not increasing in wisdom, you can experience all these things and still have a heart that is far from Him.

Without wisdom to help you set your affections on the things above, you will not be able to recalibrate your affections, live from heaven's perspective, live your message, or embrace your mission.

Wisdom is the cornerstone upon which all these others are based.

Wisdom at its heart is knowing God and pursuing His ways. There's nothing more important than to know God and pursue His ways.

> **WISDOM AT ITS HEART IS KNOWING GOD AND PURSUING HIS WAYS.**

God does not make mistakes. If you know Him and you know His ways, you are embracing wisdom that is unfailing and without fault. What could be a higher priority than knowing God and pursuing His ways?

God desires that we gain wisdom—in fact, He tells us we can ask and He will give it freely. James writes, "*If any of you lacks wisdom, let him ask of God, who gives to all liberally and without reproach, and it will be given to him*" (James 1:5). I encourage you to read in 1 Kings about how God responded to Solomon requesting wisdom instead of riches or long life—God gave Solomon every good blessing because he first pursued wisdom.

But God does not give us wisdom all at once. We gain it by spending time in His presence, and I believe that thoughts are the denomination and the method through which God gives us wisdom.

Your Thoughts Are Louder Than Words

In the previous chapter, we began by talking about examining ourselves. We could ask for no better place to begin examining our lives than our thought lives. In heaven, God's dimension, *thoughts are louder than words because thoughts reveal intrinsic nature of the soul.* The verse in Proverbs I quoted earlier tells us that as a man thinks in his heart, so is he.

The Word tells us that we are to take every thought captive and make it obedient to Christ. I showed you that you can choose your affections and therefore influence your emotions, but it is important to know that you can also take or reject thoughts.

In heaven, thoughts are louder than words because they reveal our souls—to God, our thoughts are broadcast out loud. Our thoughts and the intentions of our hearts are clear and obvious to Him. The thing is, *most of us have a part of our soul that's ugly*. Most of us have a part of our soul we keep private and not on public display. And that's the part God's going after. He's trying to capture it; He wants to remodel it, renew it, and transform it—but this is a life-long battle.

When we give Him access to our lives to search our hearts, we are giving Him access to these ugly parts of our lives. We fight a battle with our flesh that seeks to bring every part of us, including every thought, captive to Christ.

Every thought, every motivation, has an origin. We have thoughts that come from our soul, thoughts that come from our spirits, and thoughts that come from the enemy. Thoughts can be placed into your mind by the propaganda of the demonic world. We can have thoughts influenced by media and entertainment and by our own soulish desires and appetites.

Every thought has an origin, and you can *choose* to accept or reject them. Remember, you can choose what you focus on. The key is focusing in on the thoughts given by God via the Holy Spirit. Focusing on God's thoughts allows Him access to the ugly portions of our soul.

This is how we fight the battle with our flesh. We allow God to transform our minds and remodel our lives by focusing on the things above, like the Word of God. But what do you do if you are unsure if a thought is from God or not? The Bible tells us that we can know a tree by its fruit—whether the fruit is good or bad. We must learn to judge our thoughts by their nature.

Judge Everything by Its Nature

Your thoughts contain a nature. They can be from a nature of love, or a nature of lust. They can be from a nature of evil or a nature of good; hatred or forgiveness. Thoughts contain a nature, and we must learn to judge them—and everything in our lives—by their nature.

In 2 Peter 1:4 we read God has given *"us exceedingly great and precious promises, that through these you may be partakers of the divine nature, having escaped the corruption that is in the world through lust."* These promises enable you to share His divine nature and escape the world's corruption caused by human desires.

Most Christians today just want divine *forgiveness*—they don't want to grow and mature. God wants us to be partakers of divine nature to change us, to change the very core of who we are. And that requires that we learn to judge everything by its nature, including our thoughts, so that we might focus on the things that are above and not below. And how can you know what the nature is? By pursuing wisdom, which knows God and His ways. You'll know you are doing this by listening to the words that come out of your mouth.

Words

When we speak, we can think and calculate what we want the hearer to understand. Our words go through a filter, a process, before we speak them when we speak to others—and even when we speak to God. We can use our words to try to sway people and convince them, to manipulate emotions and try to get what we want.

I went to Yad Vashem Museum in Jerusalem, the Holocaust museum, and I listened to the words of a man named Adolf Hitler who was a master at propaganda and manipulating emotion. He said calculated words as a ploy to gather nationalism to destroy other nations, other people's rights, other people's identity—especially the Jewish race. He was masterful with his words. If he had gotten up at the beginning and said he wanted to put to death *all* Jewish people in concentration camps and that he wanted to put them in gas chambers and slaughter them, even their little children, it would not have worked. But his thoughts were hidden in clever words.

This is why thoughts speak louder than words in heaven—God sees us without our calculated efforts to put things the way we want them. With our mouths we can say all the right Christian things but still have hearts that are unrepentant and unregenerate—these are the parts God is after.

God does what I have urged you to learn—He judges our words by the thoughts behind them. That's why it's so important for you to take that hidden part of your soul and present it to the Lord. Your unguarded words, spoken without thinking, can be a great indicator of what is going on in your heart and whether or not you are embracing knowing Him and His ways. However, what we say when we are carefully thinking it through can tell us a lot about our spiritual condition as well and present us with a powerful tool for life transformation.

Your words are creative—they're the most creative thing you have in your life. And you must carefully judge the thoughts behind them, the nature of those thoughts, and present them before the Lord. You must ask Him to search and know the deepest, ugliest parts of your soul—the parts you want to keep hidden—because your thoughts reveal those parts to Him anyway.

A great way to judge your words and the thoughts behind them is by holding them up to the peace test. If you have peace in your heart about a thought, if you have God's peace about saying or doing something, you have a very good idea regarding its nature. We are told to "*seek peace and pursue it*" (Psalms 34:14), and if you are not at peace within yourself, it is time to check your affections and everything that flows down from there.

If you lose your peace, you lose your creativity. You do things out of reaction rather than response. You react to things rather than respond to them. You must keep peace inside of you. If you've lost your peace, check your affections—check the nature behind your thoughts.

> IF YOU'VE LOST YOUR PEACE, CHECK YOUR AFFECTIONS.

He is Jealous for Your Affections

So again we must ask God to search our hearts, and we must judge our affections and thoughts by their nature. I want to share with you something God gave me for my congregation, because it shows God's heart toward us as we seek to let Him remodel even the ugliest parts of our lives.

> *"Proceed in life with caution—remember that I'm jealous for your affections. Your life must be lived with great anticipation for My return. Let nothing pull affections away from the passion of the marriage supper of the Lamb."*

All of these thoughts on setting your affections are about building an environment that reinforces you as the betrothed of the Lord. Begin to adjust your life in the light of your union with Jesus, for we are His bride, and He desires to come back and find us remade in His image.

But He has not left us to do this on our own. He "*gave Himself for her* [the Church], *that He might sanctify and cleanse her with the washing of water by the word, that He might present her to Himself a glorious church, not having spot or wrinkle or any such thing, but that she should be holy and without blemish*" (Ephesians 5:25-27).

Like any bride, we must set our affections on our Bridegroom—His will and ways. We must pursue the things He desires us to pursue, for in having a life that is both a message and a mission, we will find greater fulfillment than we could ever dream of apart from Him. Ask Him to inhabit even the spotty and wrinkly portions of your soul, to help you judge your thoughts and affections so that you will have the wisdom to understand their nature. In choosing to focus on His things—that which is above, not below—you will find Him remaking you into the clean, mature bride He desires to return to. He who has begun a good work in you will be faithful to complete it!

So can anything interfere with that process? Can anything stop His remodeling process in your life? What about our enemy the devil—can he hinder and hamstring God's legacy-building work in your life? In the next chapter, I am going to explain that there is indeed someone and something that can derail God's purpose for your life—and these things may not be what you expect.

17

NO ROOM FOR COMPROMISE

In the previous chapters, we explored the importance of asking God to examine our hearts and how vital it is that we set our affections on Him. We talked about your life mission and the fact that He knows your thoughts, and at the end of the previous chapter, I told you that there is someone and something that can derail God's purpose for your life. Don't believe me? Let's talk about what happens when a Christian embraces something so insidious and destructive that it can ruin God's dream for your life.

Before I talk about a mortal threat to the legacy God has for your life, first I want to tell you about what God has provided to prevent it—His Word. Without a solid foundation built upon God's Word, the only universal truth man has ever found, we cannot build and establish lives that will leave a lasting legacy on the earth.

The Word of God must establish your life personally—you must be firmly rooted on God's immutable principles. Other things may contribute to your life and help you grow and develop, but the Word of God must be the foundation upon which you build everything else. If you do not build with God's Word as a solid foundation, everything you use to construct your life will come crashing down. For without a foundation of the Word, you are building on shifting sands—the shifting sands of compromise.

At the heart of the issue is that we human beings have an amazing ability to accept *compromise* in its many forms. We can rationalize almost anything. We are all too often open to a spirit of compromise on the very issues that we should never negotiate—but if we negotiate on our principles, we are not people of integrity. And if we embrace compromise, we ourselves can become the greatest threat to the legacy God desires for us to leave behind to our children.

> **WE ARE ALL TOO OFTEN OPEN TO A SPIRIT OF COMPROMISE ON THE VERY ISSUES THAT WE SHOULD NEVER NEGOTIATE.**

Compromise Comes Camouflaged

God's Word must be our foundation, and we must never compromise on His commands. However, the trouble is that rarely does compromise seek to enter our lives blatantly and obviously. It does not announce its presence in a way that alerts us to its life-destroying presence; it sneaks in around the edges of our lives.

Compromise enters subtly—it comes camouflaged as something that seems so reasonable, so understandable. And if you have not embraced God's Word and His precepts, you can be ambushed by compromise disguised as something that did not obviously threaten your Christian principles.

Let us take a look together at some of the ways that compromise camouflages itself in order to be better prepared to expose it to the light of God's truth. We will begin with looking at how easily we can rationalize compromise in our lives.

We Live in an Age of Reason

The Bible tells us that the carnal, fleshly mind cannot receive the things of God, for they are spiritually discerned. Our rational mind can't comprehend God, for He is spiritual, so if we rely solely on our rational minds, we can easily find ourselves rationalizing compromise in a way that is very dangerous.

Now, God gave us our minds that we might think and comprehend. We show a great deal of similarity to our Creator because we possess the ability to imagine that which is not and then build and create it. But if we only rely on our rational mind, we will limit ourselves from comprehending the things of God.

Proverbs says, "*Trust in the LORD with all your heart, and lean not on your own understanding*" (Proverbs 3:5). When we fail to do this, we open ourselves to the spirit of compromise.

Human beings can rationalize nearly anything. People can come to see a new life as an inconvenience, not a person. We can rationalize away God's commands about sexuality because our culture is so permissive, not understanding that His definitions about sex and marriage are there for our good, not to ruin our freedom. Name a divisive issue within our culture, and I guarantee that the truth in God's Word is unpopular and seen as repressive.

God did not give us His guiding commands to stifle us; He gave them to protect us. When we defy them, it injures us. We need years of help and healing to overcome the grief of abortion, the emotional scarring of casual sex, or compromising on any of God's precepts.

Yet as a culture, we have rationalized away the godly foundation we once had. We have lifted up our ability to reason, and we have made the Word of God outmoded by our supposedly enlightened understanding.

In truth, people have replaced the things of God, which as I have said the rational mind does not understand, with the best human beings can come up with. Our compromise has caused human thought to outweigh the authority of God Himself. And the result of this over-reliance on rational thinking is hurting lost generations who do not even know about God's ways.

God's Ways are Unreasonable

We begin to cover this in the previous point—that human rational thought is supplanting God's outdated restrictions. Compromise can enter our lives under the guise that the Bible and what God says are "unreasonable."

It is downright unreasonable of God to say that marriage is restricted to just certain people who love each other. It is unreasonable that you should not have as many sexual partners as you desire. It is unreasonable that you should make your children obey or come to church. Or so say the "rational thinkers" of our society. To them, the Word of God is repressive.

I will not deny that the Bible puts restrictions on behaviors. But God's laws are not arbitrary, and more accurately we should say they are *restraining*. God's principles are restraining devices for our lives.

If you have ever ridden a rollercoaster, you can appreciate the fact that some narrow-minded, repressive engineer decided to build a rollercoaster with something as limiting to your freedom as a "restraining device." How dare he decide that he knows what is best for all the various people who might ride that rollercoaster! How dare he decide what is right for everyone else!

And who gave the right to automobile manufactures to put seat belts and airbags in their cars? And why should the government be able to tell us we *must* wear these seatbelts? Should we not have our personal freedom?

These are of course absurd examples, but if you look at God's Word with the simple understanding that He is the Engineer who designed humanity and understands us best, it is not so unreasonable after all that He would create principles to preserve our safety.

Would you ride a rollercoaster with no restraining devices? If not, why would you want to live your life without the restraining devices that your Creator designed for your good? Now *that* is unreasonable!

I'm Just Fitting In

Compromise often camouflages itself within our desire to fit in with others. Nearly all people feel this intrinsic desire to fit in with those around us, and nearly all of us deal with the spirit of rejection that can motivate us to compromise on even the most important components of our lives because of this desire to be accepted. Yet if we live our lives based on the desire to fit in with others, we can easily allow the spirit of rejection to dictate our lives, which is a recipe for living a life of compromise.

We must not trade the favor of God for the acceptance of man. Never has a life more exemplified this than that of Jesus Christ. Jesus came to do the Father's will, and He was rejected nearly everywhere He went. Even His own disciples rejected Him when He was taken in the Garden of Gethsemane. John 1:11 says, "*He came to His own, and His own did not receive Him.*"

Even Jesus' own creation did not accept Him, and we must not let the pressure to fit in deceive us into thinking that the world will treat us any differently than it treated Him. Later in the Gospel of John, Jesus explains that if the world rejects us, remember that it hated Him first.

Do not expect to be accepted when you stand for God's principles, particularly in this day and age. Yet Jesus willingly came to this earth and sacrificed Himself for people who hated Him. Why did He do this? It's quite simple—love.

We, too, must understand the great love that God has for every person, and we must recognize that God has put us here to lead them to Him regardless of whether or not we feel accepted. Someone must lead, but to be a godly leader, you must follow God and His principles closely and without compromise. Your entire life is a letter to those who are unsaved, Paul tells us. When you walk in the integrity of the Word of God, your very existence is a testimony.

God Will Understand

We live under the grace of the New Covenant—grace that Jesus' blood purchased for us on Calvary. Yet all too often we do fail to understand that grace is not God turning a blind eye to our failure to keep the law; if anything, it is a call to a higher standard.

> GOD DOES NOT MAKE EXCUSES FOR OUR DISOBEDIENCE, AND NEITHER SHOULD WE.

I hear people and even preachers saying that because God loves us He will "understand" when we fall short or compromise—in other words, that He will let it slide like some permissive grandfather in heaven. But God is not a grandfather who wishes to spoil us; He is a Father who wishes to create children who are like Him.

God does not "understand" in the way these people mean. Let me tell you something—Jesus was tempted in every way, yet in all points, He was without sin. God does not "understand," He provides a way of escape from temptation! Do these people who preach a permissive God not know that the Bible tells us we will be judged according to the deeds we have done? Yes, those who put their trust in Christ have salvation, but we will also be held accountable. God does not make excuses for our disobedience, and neither should we.

The Devil Made Me Do It

Compromise camouflages itself by creating questions about who is responsible for our actions. You have no doubt heard someone say that it was not his fault but the way he was reared that caused him to do a certain thing. The message here is, "It's not my fault. I'm not really responsible for my actions."

The temptation to shift responsibility from our own shoulders on to literally anything else is very common in our culture, and it is one of the primary ways compromise can slip into our lives. We feel that if there are mitigating factors contributing to why we do a certain thing or fail to do it, the results are not really our fault.

These failures can be sins of omission and commission. There are sins of what we fail to do—we may omit prayer or tithing from our lives—and sins that we do actively, such as lying or giving place to lust. People rationalize these sins because of their backgrounds, and in so doing, they allow compromise into their lives. Yet the truest form of faith in God is obedience to His Word, and the Word of God leaves no room for compromise on His principles.

God created us with a will—the ability to choose. Adam and Eve chose to disobey God in the Garden of Eden, and we human beings have been making sinful choices ever since. God does not make us sin or ever tempt us to sin, and no temptation that we experience is outside of Jesus' experience or beyond God's ability to deliver us.

When we allow compromise to enter our lives by shifting blame and responsibility, we are being double-minded—saying that we are Christians and believe God, yet denying His power to deliver us from temptation. When we are double-minded, we will not receive from the Lord. We must reject compromise and blame-shifting, and decide to take responsibility for our own actions by repenting and selling out completely to God. We must believe that what the Word says is true and act on it by being uncompromising, no matter the mitigating factors in our lives.

God is greater than the way you were reared, and He is greater than the scars life has given you. You have the ability to choose, and if you wish to leave a legacy, you must choose not to compromise on the principles of God's Word.

I'm a Victim

Closely related to the last point is the idea that we are just victims of evil influences. "I'm just a victim here," some people say. This can have *some* truth in it; we can be victims when we have been victimized. Children lose their innocence in our society far earlier than ever before, and we may be victimized by witnessing or experiencing lust or violence, which can scar us from an early age.

However, adults are still responsible for our choices. In fact, your life is the result of the choices you made, and after the immediate events of your victimization—when it is over—you face a decision of whether or not to *live* as a victim.

God tells us to tithe, and if we do not tithe, it is disobedience. He tells us to be witnesses for Him, and if we do not witness, this is a choice to disobey. We are told to forgive, to pray, and to do so many other things that *we fail to do*. Similarly, the Word tells us *not* to do many things that we do. We must take responsibility for these actions and repent—turn from them and toward God—and reject compromise or excuses, no matter the bad things that may have happened to us.

Yet some people might say that because they are victims they have a "weakness" in an area—as though that "weakness" is too great for God's redemptive, life-changing power. Instead of taking responsibility and repenting, they compromise. Remember from the early part of this book: *your weakness is not wickedness, but you cannot make excuses for your weakness or live in it.*

We rationalize our obedience away. We say that it is unreasonable for us to tithe—we don't have much money because we were raised in poverty. We tell ourselves we're not good speakers because we never learned how, so God's call to witness is more for someone else—someone with a pulpit. We justify away unforgiveness because we think the circumstances that hurt us are special or unique, or we excuse ourselves from prayer because of the busy lifestyle our jobs demand.

In these ways and many others, compromise camouflages itself in order to enter our lives. But identifying the spirit of compromise's tactics is only the first step in dealing with it. Next, I want to look at where compromise really begins. It is not outside pressure, as some think; compromise actually begins in our hearts.

Outward Failure is the Result of Inward Compromise

We have all seen the very public failure of noteworthy people in the Church and society at large—the news is full of scandals. Yet we must understand that no man fails outwardly unless he first fails *inwardly*. All of the failures that we see publicly really began with an internal struggle. They began with a spirit of compromise.

No one wakes up one morning and arbitrarily says, "I think I'll cheat on my spouse today," or "I think I'll lie to the ones I love today." We do not suddenly and unexpectedly move into outward sin without first having inner struggles with the spirit of compromise.

> **NO MAN FAILS OUTWARDLY UNLESS HE FIRST FAILS INWARDLY.**

The Bible helps us see that even the people in the Word were human, just like you and me. David, a man after God's own heart, failed spectacularly—yet he repented and God kept His covenant to David's offspring. Joshua failed to completely destroy some of Israel's enemies as commanded, but God stopped the sun in the sky when Joshua prayed to Him.

But we can also see examples from the lives of the men and women in the Bible who possessed a spirit of uncompromising obedience and faith in God. These individuals did not compromise in difficult outward situations because they had rejected the spirit of inward compromise.

To me, Daniel is one of the greatest examples of a man with the ability to deal rightly with the spirit of compromise. In the first chapter of Daniel, we read of his conviction: *"But Daniel purposed in his heart that he would not defile himself with the portion of the king's delicacies, nor with the wine which he drank; therefore he requested of the chief of the eunuchs that he might not defile himself"* (Daniel 1:8).

He knew that the king's aim was to subvert Daniel and his Hebrew companions to his pagan ways, and diet was just one of the ways Daniel could have compromised. He had to resist a direct order of the king to resist the spirit of compromise, and it would not be the last time Daniel and his friends had to go against the strongest pressure to compromise possible—they literally risked death to obey God and His principles.

It may seem so unreasonable to us that Daniel refused to eat the choice foods at the king's table—many of us would have said that this was a blessing! While the rest of the Jews were scratching by in captivity, Daniel could eat T-bones. Surely that was God's favor . . . except that Daniel saw this was the spirit of compromise *disguised* as a blessing. He understood that disobeying God's rules on his Jewish diet was just the first step the king wanted him to take that would have seen Daniel down a path far from God's will for him.

Understand this: If you think you are being blessed for compromising on something God has said, it is not a blessing of the Lord. In fact, it will actually be a *curse*. The first compromise may be small, and it may be inward, in your heart. But terrible outward destruction is the result of compromise that begins seemingly quietly and insignificantly. Instead, we must take the lives of people like Daniel as examples and refuse to compromise on even the smallest element of God's principles. In so doing, we will stay aware and sensitive to the witness of God's Holy Spirit.

Compromise Desensitizes

Compromise is so insidious because it desensitizes us to sin. We think it is just one little thing that we are bending on, but it is just the first step in a gradual—and sometimes not so gradual!—slide away from God's good and perfect will for our lives.

To me, our entertainment is an excellent barometer for how desensitized we have become. What kind of shows do you watch on TV that you would not have watched when you were closer with God? What kinds of things do you allow in your life because of the good acting, engaging story, or other rationalization that you would not have felt comfortable watching before? Your entertainment is a great test to show you where your heart is and whether or not you are becoming desensitized.

> **C**OMPROMISE IS SO INSIDIOUS BECAUSE IT DESENSITIZES US TO SIN.

Compromising on God's principles starts small, but it leads to major destruction. It can literally destroy your soul. The devil will not start with his most blatant, obvious attacks first—he will insinuate compromise slowly and gradually, desensitizing you to sin and unrighteousness. And that is a slippery slope once you have started down it!

Tolerance

The world has a term for this slide of moral principle into compromise: they call it being "tolerant." They even have the audacity to call it a *virtue*. Society wants us to be tolerant of everything, claiming that tolerance is synonymous with *love*.

We are to be tolerant of other people's behavior—their language, their sexual practices and lifestyle, their religion. We are to tolerate everything about other people (even when they are hypocritically intolerant of Christians). After all, we live in a morally subjective culture where whatever works for you is okay for you, and what works for me is what works for me—except that is *not* what God says! God says there are absolutes and that there is *one right way*—His way.

One "tolerance" that bothers me intensely is swearing and using the Lord's name as a curse. Someone once shouted out the name of the Lord Jesus as a curse near me, and I said, "Oh, you know Him too?"

But we have become conditioned to thinking that this man's vocabulary is subjectively right for him and that we should be tolerant. The real danger is when it no longer bothers us, because this is a strong indication that we have become desensitized. If you find yourself tolerant of things that defy God's Word, it is time to ask Him for heart surgery, because desensitization has dulled your heart and spirit to God's ways and principles.

God does not want a bride for Christ that is tolerant and blemished with compromise; He desires to take our hard, rationalizing hearts and clean us up so He can show His glory to the earth through us. He desires to make us containers of His anointing and blessing so we can minister to a lost and hurting world.

But first He must clean our containers; first He must remake our hearts after His. He needs to remove the sickness of compromise that plagues us by anointing us with the fresh oil and wine of the Holy Spirit.

Compromise and the Spirit of Mockery

The spirit of compromise is synonymous with the spirit of mockery. Galatians 6:7 says, "*Do not be deceived, God is not mocked; for whatever a man sows, that he will also reap.*" When we compromise yet still expect God to bless us, we are mocking God —we are saying that we understand He has principles and statutes but that our case is special. We are saying that He should treat us by unique,

> **W**HEN WE COMPROMISE YET STILL EXPECT GOD TO BLESS US, WE ARE MOCKING GOD

adjusted standards, because we acknowledge there is a godly standard and yet make choices and excuses for not living up to them in the power of the Holy Spirit.

This attitude mocks God, and we will indeed reap what we sow. We are not exempt because of special circumstances; we are not special cases. We are His children just like any other, and He expects us to obey His commands if we are indeed really His children.

I mentioned consequences earlier, and here is when they come into play: if you insist on being treated as a special case by allowing compromise into your life, you are mocking God. And He will allow the consequences of your actions to act like a spiritual spanking! The Lord disciplines those He loves, and He will allow you to reap consequences when you compromise because He wants you to accept His correction and let that compromise be disciplined right out of your life.

Our lives must become the signature of Jesus, a letter to a lost and dying world. When we compromise, we are not bringing God glory.

Just who out in the world is worth emulating, anyway? Look at the people our society holds in high esteem—musicians, actors, business people, and politicians, to name a few. Their children are confused disasters, their marriages end in shambles, and they turn to drugs and alcohol in misguided attempts to quench the pain in their lives.

And yet Jesus-professing Christians will compromise on God's standards to emulate these very people! We are not to model or live like the supposedly successful individuals of this world—we are to emulate the life of Christ. We must try to be like Jesus in every way as God changes us from glory to glory to resemble the image of our Savior.

Our culture—even the Church—is rife with compromise. It infests our lives like a disease. So what is the cure? God gave the Law to show that we could not live up to His standard on our own, so what are we to do? In the next chapter, I will give you the antidote for compromise—the question is, will you take it?

18
GOD'S ANTIDOTE

You may be wondering what we can do when God reveals the corruption of compromise in our lives. Well, obviously we cannot fix ourselves—we never could, for the righteousness of man is nothing like the righteousness of God.

The antidote for the spirit of compromise is the fear of the Lord. Christians should be the ones resisting compromise and standing for principles, for we have a fear of the Lord operating in our lives. If we will embrace this reverence and awe for God, which He so eminently deserves, it will absolutely deal with the spirit of compromise.

> **THE ANTIDOTE FOR THE SPIRIT OF COMPROMISE IS THE FEAR OF THE LORD.**

But what, you may be asking, is the fear of the Lord? You may have heard this term used in Christian circles, but what does it really mean, and how do we actively employ it in our lives? Let us look together at some aspects of the fear of the Lord, for as I said, it is the chief way we can deal with this insidious spirit of compromise—the only way that will work.

Reverential Fear Comes from Honor and Love

The fear of the Lord is reverential fear that comes from a heart of love and honor. Many people think that the fear of the Lord is being afraid that God will literally blast them out of the water or squash them like a bug for angering Him. This view comes from an incorrect notion about God. Yes, there will be a day of judgment, and we will stand accountable for what we did with the knowledge of Christ. Did we turn to Him? Did we place our faith in Him? But that day is not here yet, and God is not in the business of blasting people with lightning.

While we do not fear a capricious, angry God, we *should* be in awe of the incomparable Creator of the universe. We should be humbled and reverent before God all-powerful, for unlike the people we may aim to please who can only affect our mortal bodies, God will separate His sheep from the goats on the Day of Judgment. When we respect and give reverence to the Lord as those who follow His voice—His sheep—we will find that honoring God will not permit you to coexist with compromise.

We all fear something. Some of us fear the opinions of men. But when you have reverential fear of the Lord, you will not give in because you love and honor Him. The Holy Spirit within you will give you the power to resist compromise, because He desires our lives to bring glory to His name.

Reverential Fear and Consequences

Reverential fear for the Lord derives its power from understanding both positive and negative consequences of obedience and disobedience. We not only honor the Lord, but we also must fear the consequences of our actions.

We might think that God's mercy will protect us, but it is vital that we understand sin has dire consequences in our lives. A minister of the gospel may fall and have an affair; if he repents and turns from his sin, the Lord will forgive him. But there will be consequences! Consequences in his home and between him and his wife; consequences within the body he led; and consequences in the Church as a whole, for his actions did not glorify God and in fact did great damage. God will give this repentant man grace *through* these circumstances, but his actions will have created significant pain in untold numbers of people.

Giving place to compromise is not just about us. Compromising can create ripples of consequences that spread out from us like a rock dropped on still waters, and the pain of our consequences is not God's fault. In fact, it can be a mercy that He allows us to experience the consequences of our actions when we grow from them and learn not to compromise.

Reverential Fear Shows in Our Lives

We show the fruit of our reverential fear of God in our lives when our tastes, desires, and values reflect the nature of Christ. This fear holds in check our own sinful nature, which does not honor God, and replaces it with a godly nature that brings glory to His name.

God created us in His likeness, but we represent Him with our choices. Our bodies are the temple of the Holy Spirit, and what we do with them reflects back on Him. If you are a Christian, you are not your own. You have been bought with a price—the precious blood of Jesus.

Reverential fear of the Lord lets us live with the knowledge that we live for Christ, but for us dying is actually *gain*. What can mere mortals do to us? Our fleshly desires and the pressure of this world pale in comparison to the joy that is before us. If we are thinking of eternity and being guided by our understanding that this life is just a starting-off point, we can subjugate our fleshly, prideful desires to the will of the Holy Spirit. When the Spirit guides your life, He will keep compromise in check and let God's glory show in your life.

Paul puts it so clearly: "*For to be carnally minded is death, but to be spiritually minded is life and peace*" (Romans 8:6). When we do it our way, we are forging ahead toward death; but when we are spiritually minded and do it God's way, we forge a legacy of life and peace.

Overcoming Compromise

Reverential fear is the antidote for compromise, and the Bible tells us that fear of the Lord is the beginning of wisdom. But what else can we do to overcome the spirit of compromise in our lives? I want to give you a few tools that will help you emulate Christ in ways that will allow you to leave a godly legacy.

1. Develop Deep Intimacy with the Father

I believe one of the first ways we overcome compromise is in the same vein as reverential fear—developing a deeper intimacy with the Father. For some time now it has been popular to imagine that God is all about *us*, that He is our buddy and friend. But this leaves out the reverential awe for the Creator of heaven and earth that should inflect our relationship with the Father.

Another element to this is the casual "fire insurance" nature with which many people pursue their faith. They just want to go to heaven, so they come down an aisle, offer a prayer, and then go about their regular lives. But God so desires intimacy with us that He sacrificed His only Son! He has held nothing back from us.

We must pursue a deeper relationship with God—a closeness and intimacy. We must seek to hear His Holy Spirit and allow our lives to be directed by eternity. If we witness His desire for intimacy, accept His salvation, and then walk away from that intimacy, it is blasphemy.

Living a life of casual compromise like that is not God's plan for your life, but the converse is true: living in close intimacy with God will help you overcome compromise in your life.

2. Judge Your Motives

If you wish to deal with compromise in your life, you must guard your heart by judging the motives behind your every action, as we have talked about elsewhere. Remember how David prayed, "*Search me, O God, and know my heart: try me, and know my thoughts*" (Psalms 139:23 KJV)? This should be the cry of our own hearts, because He is offering to prevent compromise before it starts!

Your motives are so important. Our spirits understand that we reap what we sow, but if we only give with a motivation to receive, we have already missed the point. We must guard our hearts even when doing something good, such as giving, for if we are doing something that appears godly but with corrupt motives, compromise has already slipped in. Guard your heart at all times, for out of it flow the issues of life.

3. Keep Your Eyes on the Prize

How do you overcome compromise? Keep your eyes on the prize —that which really matters. Someday we will all stand before Jesus, and when we live with our eyes on eternity instead of the here and now, it keeps our values fixed on what truly matters. This will help prevent our eyes latching onto the passing, trivial things of this world and will allow us to do right. When we walk in righteousness, God can bless that nature. And I would rather have an ounce of God's blessing on my life than compromise on a little thing and receive millions of dollars for it. Is the insignificant thing you are thinking about compromising on God's standards really worth it in the light of eternity? I think not!

4. Cherish the Word of God

As a whole, Christians take the Word far too casually. We think the Bible is full of suggestions or general principles. While it does have general principles, it is full of the instructions God Himself desires His people to obey! The Word is mighty and powerful; it is substance and reality when all the other voices around us are only smoke and mirrors.

Not long ago I traveled to Israel, and while there and on the flights, I saw devout Jews praying and reading the Torah. Jewish men wear little braided tassels on the edge of their garments to represent the Word of God, keeping the reminder always close by. When they pray, they are intense and deeply sincere. When they handle the Torah, the Word, they are reverent, even just with the book itself.

What if, like a devout Jew, when we got ready in the morning it was full of the reminders of God's principles? What if, as they do, we prayed, "God, keep me from breaking any of Your commandments," instead of asking, "God, thank You for Your grace for the commandment I'm about to break"?

When we treat God's principles as options, we are treating His Word lightly, and we are not cherishing it. In Psalm 119, David repeatedly sings his praises of the Word, saying that God's law is his delight. If you wish to know what cherishing the Word is like, I challenge you to read this psalm through and search out David's love for God's Word and ask God to give you the same passion.

5. *Understand Your Mission*

Your life has a purpose, and when you understand your life's mission, you will be better able to resist compromise because of that vision set before you. Your life *is* a mission—and your mission is to touch people with the gospel of Jesus Christ.

> **W**HEN YOU UNDERSTAND YOUR LIFE'S MISSION, YOU WILL BE BETTER ABLE TO RESIST COMPROMISE.

The Bible tells us that God ordained and predestined us to do good works, but that does not mean that Christians who compromise will see the fullness of this mission. If you are living casually instead of being directed by God's decrees and Holy Spirit, the mission God has for you may have to pass to someone else. But when you live with an understanding that your life is a mission to the world, you can resist the compromise that wishes to make that mission a failure.

6. Remember What Jesus Went Through

If you want to resist the spirit of compromise, remember what Jesus experienced as He refused to compromise on God's mission for His life. Most of us will never experience a fraction of what Christ endured as He went to and endured the cross. We may be mocked for our "outdated" beliefs or feel as though we do not fit in, but our Lord Jesus was beaten so badly that you could not even recognize Him.

When the spirit of compromise entices you to negotiate on God's principles, remember that the Lord Jesus Christ *never* compromised so that He could give you the gift of eternal life. We have the mind of Christ, the Bible says, and we have the same Holy Spirit power working in us for life and godliness that raised Christ from the dead. You can resist compromise because of what Jesus accomplished on the cross and the Helper He sent to be with us every moment of every day!

7. Listen to the Holy Spirit

The same Spirit that came down and rested on Jesus in the form of a dove and which He gave to us at Pentecost is with every Christian who welcomes Him. His voice is still and small, but we can train our spiritual ears to discern it even amid the louder voices of this world that urge us to compromise.

Before you bend and break God's principles, stop! Be still—and listen for the voice of the Holy Spirit's conviction. The Bible tells us that it is His job to convict of sin—and this is not guilt or condemnation. The Holy Spirit brings conviction that what we are about to do or have done is wrong and not part of God's plan for us. Conviction is your friend! Listen to His voice, and turn from compromise.

8. Develop a Heart of Humility

I believe that often we compromise because we are thinking only of ourselves in that moment. This selfishness and pride that urges us to leave behind God's restraining devices and compromise causes us to ignore the effect our actions will have on those around us.

A heart of humility urges us to resist compromise not only for the sake of our own souls but because it blemishes the name of the Lord Jesus. It harms our families, makes our Christian brothers stumble, and casts all believers in a poorer light for unbelievers. It is not all about you—your choices can deeply impact those around you. For their sakes as well as your own, you must learn to walk in humility and overcome the spirit of compromise.

Overcome Compromise to Leave a Legacy of Righteousness

The spirit of compromise will destroy your destiny. It will keep you from receiving the blessings of the Lord. With it come heaviness, depression, anxiety, and lack of peace. Compromising on God's will and principles is like riding the rollercoaster of life with no restraining devices, and tragedy will strike when we let the spirit of compromise take us off the tracks God intends for our lives.

I urge you to fall in love with God's Word—His laws and statutes reveal His character and the best possible path for our lives. Cherishing God's Word and listening to the voice of the Holy Spirit will reveal compromise however it may camouflage itself. A life of integrity lived to honor God will shine brighter and brighter in a world of negotiated principles.

Overcoming the spirit of compromise will leave behind a legacy of righteousness to future generations—a life that others can look at and respect and which points glory back at our God and Father. You may not know this, but your life itself is a test. This earth, this life, is not all there is. The legacy you leave on earth will follow you into eternity, and this life is your chance to let God so renew you that you can end strong and influence future generations. So let us take this next chapter to look more closely at this test He gives us.

19
LIFE IS GOD'S TEST

I want to share an important understanding with you that I pray is not just words on a page, but is a message that speaks to the very soul of who you are. Many people wonder what life is all about, and while I strongly believe that each of us has a divine mission, our lives also have another significance in our walk with God. Every event of our lives is an opportunity for us to show God how we will respond. This has been the case since the patriarchs of the Bible, and it is still true today.

Abraham's life is a great example of this: God gave him the chance to show his faith. We read in Genesis that God tested and proved Abraham (see Genesis 22:1). God was about to ask Abraham to sacrifice his only son—the son of his promise from God—and Abraham took it to the very edge. He had the wood piled, had put the boy on the altar, and the knife was in his hand. Abraham was ready to obey God even in this and was about to bring the knife down—when God stopped him.

God provided a sacrificial ram, sparing Isaac's life, because He did not truly desire Abraham's son as a sacrifice. He was doing something quite different: testing Abraham. Life is God's test.

The Scripture is quite clear that God was testing *and* approving Abraham and his faith. It is very important for you as a believer to understand that God tests us. God uses every victory, every challenge, and every failure as a test to observe you and see how you respond.

You see, we can all make the right Christian sounds in church. But life's trials—and even our victories—reveal what we *really* have in our hearts. We all have a secret, hidden side—the deep places of our hearts—that God is searching and testing, as we examined earlier. He desires that we show ourselves approved, but He cannot get us to respond from the innermost parts of our being while we are just sitting in a pew worshiping. We reveal what is really inside us under pressure, and in these times, life's trials are the tests God uses to reveal the real you.

> LIFE'S TRIALS ARE THE TESTS GOD USES TO REVEAL THE REAL YOU.

He tests us not only in the hard times, however, but also in our victories. He wants to see if we will respond in a godly manner when we win and not just when times are hard. I have seen victory cause more ruin than failure because people's pride and ego can become mingled with the blessings of God.

God tests us to see how consumed and committed we are with His desire for our lives.

God Gives His Wisdom to Those Who Obey

I want to tell you something that may shock you: God does not give His wisdom and vision to passive people. Who is a passive person? It is the person who wants to do something for God but doesn't want to do the *work* that is necessary. These people may receive the command—God's vision or dream for their lives—but they do not obey.

God expects that you will be activated by every vision or drop of wisdom He gives—and will obey Him. He does not want you to simply talk about what He has given you—He wants you to *act* on it! If you have received a vision and dream from God, you are assigned to make it happen. If you do not, He will go no further and will not give you more wisdom or vision, because you have not obeyed. God does not give His wisdom and vision to you if you are passive with them.

Abraham showed this so clearly with the story of nearly sacrificing Isaac, but it would be a mistake to think that Abraham suddenly woke up one day with a mandate from God to sacrifice his son after never hearing from Him before. God first called Abraham (then Abram) out of his father's house in Ur. His father was not a believer in Jehovah God, and in fact, he was surrounded by idols. His first act of obedience to God was to leave his father and everything he was familiar with, including his inheritance, and follow God—and God had not even told him the final destination!

Hebrews tells us that even though Abraham did not know where he was going, he went out in faith. This kind of faith walk contains an element of adventure that should thrill every believer! Our God is a God of adventure, but we only live that adventure when we are active and obedient in stepping out when He tells us what we should do. Christians are called the "Children of Abraham," and this sense of adventure is as surely a part of our birthright as is salvation. The question is, will we have faith as Abraham did to step out and obey, or will we be passive and stay with our idols?

The Real Promise

After Abraham stepped out in faith and left his father's house, God saw that he had passed a test. God was ready to make Abraham a far greater promise than simply leading him to a better neighborhood—a land filled with milk and honey. After he had followed God to the Lord's destination, Abraham received the promise that God would make him a mighty nation by giving him a son, even in his old age.

We often gloss over the years and years that passed between God's initial promise to make a great nation of Abraham and Isaac's birth. Abraham didn't pass this waiting test as well as he did God's assignment to leave his father, and Ishmael is the evidence. But years later when God told Abraham to take his son of promise to Mount Moriah and sacrifice him there, Abraham had learned. And he obeyed.

You see, God wanted to test Abraham's godliness and faith in the face of having received the promise—He wanted to see how Abraham responded to *victory*, not just failure. God never wanted *Isaac*—God wanted *Abraham*!

God wanted his heart.

It was always a test, but in Abraham's mind, he had decided to sacrifice his son if that was what God asked. Even though God stayed his hand at the moment of impact, God knew that Abraham passed the ultimate test.

Abraham had acted on God's instructions many times, but it was in passing this test that Abraham showed God's blessing had not gone to his head and that he was faithful to God's covenant with him. After all, Abraham was willing to offer his son of promise, and it is right that God offered His only Son through Abraham's bloodline.

This Life Counts for Eternity

When we receive instruction from God and do not obey and act on it, we are like the unprofitable servant who buried the talent his lord had given him instead of using it or at least investing it wisely. When his lord returned, he took what he had given to this unfruitful servant and gave it to one who had been acting on what he'd received and was obeying.

If we are too passive, we may be tempted to think that our lives here do not count for anything. Yet each one of us must understand that our lives count for eternity—we will be held to account for how we use them. God has something of eternal value that you are to accomplish in the land of the living—a life mission, as we've talked about in other chapters—and God is going to test you along the way. With each test comes new vision and deeper wisdom from Him, but when we do not obey and fail the test, we stop receiving vision and wisdom until we repent and obey.

> **WITH EACH TEST COMES NEW VISION AND DEEPER WISDOM**

Every test requires faith. Provision for stepping out in obedience does not follow you; it *awaits* your obedience. Every single assignment God has given me has preceded the provision to accomplish it. I did not have it in my hand when He gave me His assignment or vision. *As I stepped out*, the provision came.

I have found that it is very difficult to lead people who lack vision, because the vast majority of people are stuck in the neutral state of reasoning and calculation. They are waiting to see the proof God is in it before they will step out and obey, and it is no surprise that these people lack God's vision and wisdom—they are stuck because they failed His obedience test.

You may recall from earlier in the book that I at one point pastored my father's church. However, because the members of the board had known me as a younger man, they had difficulty accepting the vision God gave me for the church and moving by faith. They were not evil people; they simply did not share my faith to step forward on these things and sacrifice to create a vision.

If I had come to them with money in hand, I am sure they would have approved many of the assignments I knew God had given me. But instead I walked into the room with a multi-million dollar vision and only loose change in my pocket, and they could not step out because they were waiting on the provision. They did not know the provision was waiting for them. Friend, we must move first and obey; then God will follow with the provision.

The Truest Test of Faith is Obedience

Abraham obeyed God *first*—without understanding. He trusted God, and he stepped out in faith. He was ready to put on the altar the most precious thing he could ever have. It is the same with all the heroes of faith we read about in Hebrews chapter eleven. Over and over, God makes promises, and those who step out in faith and obey are those who receive more of His vision and wisdom—even when it is their children who live to see the promises come to pass.

When God gives you thoughts, visions, dreams, and assignments from Him and you obey, He's ready to give you more. When you put it up on the shelf and wait for everything to work out right so you can start . . . you won't get another one until you repent. You have to move with the information God has given you, whether you see it in the natural or not. This is the faith walk.

Life is a test. You are being tested every single day that you live, and you must realize that obedience is not an option. You are either obedient or disobedient.

Now, some may argue that God will forgive you for your disobedience. But hang on a moment—God forgives based upon *repentance*. Repentance means turning around and going the other way, turning from your sin. It means going to the spot where you disobeyed—and making it right by obedience.

Every Christian has something God has shown us but we failed to act upon and obey. We've received revelation about projects and outreaches and missions, and some wonder why God never carried out that dream and vision. However, it is not God's fault—it is ours. When we fail to step out in obedience, nothing happens. If you show me a Christian with a ministry God is using, I will show you an obedient person who stepped out in faith.

The Bible tells us that when we draw near to God, He draws near to us. You see, our action on earth precedes the action of heaven. How so? When you take a step of obedience to God's vision, He does not just match you—He takes *two*. If you will take two steps, He will take four. You cannot out-give God, and when we obey, He goes before us to ensure His Word does not return void.

Just as every day of life is a test, so too is every day an opportunity to glimpse the eternal capacity God has placed in you. As you obey, He gives you more vision and wisdom, and He desires to show you how to apply them toward your life mission. He has a great desire to do something through your life that will follow you into eternity and give Him glory.

Your Obedience Determines Your Vessel

Many people are visionless because they have failed to obey. They are waiting for their human understanding to confirm what God has said—they are waiting for the provision before they act on the vision. As long as you let fear or uncertainty hold you back, God will not trust you with more vision for your life. You must first be tested and show yourself approved—then you will receive more. The key, then, to receiving the next steps of God's assignment is obeying the assignment you have received.

Many times God will speak to you about one small, little thing that you either catch or miss, but if you catch it and obey it, it can turn into something magnificent and have an eternal impact. God can use your obedience to step out in one small act of mercy and love to ignite a movement, to establish His heart in the earth, and to make something count for eternity. You must learn to obey Him even in the

> MANY PEOPLE ARE VISIONLESS BECAUSE THEY HAVE FAILED TO OBEY.

little things, for if you do not obey in the small things, He will not entrust you with the larger ones.

It's important to move beyond the arena of human comfort. Listen to the voice of the Holy Spirit; be alert to what God is trying to speak to you. When you obey, you are helping to determine what kind of vessel you are in God's kingdom.

We read in 2 Timothy 2:20, *"But in a great house there are not only vessels of gold and silver, but also of wood and clay, some for honor and some for dishonor."* Other translations say that there are vessels for special use and others for common use. Paul goes on to say, *"Therefore if anyone cleanses himself from the latter, he will be a vessel for honor, sanctified and useful for the Master, prepared for every good work"* (2 Timothy 2:21).

So what kind of vessel are you? If you are saved, you're a vessel in God's house. But it is in obeying and passing God's tests that we become vessels of honor for special use. If you wish to be a vessel of honor and leave a legacy to your children and their children, you must ask yourself something very important: is ambition driving you, or does honor provide your drive?

20

DRIVEN BY HONOR

What motivated Abraham? Was it vain ambition, ego, and pride? Or was it something else? I would argue that rather than these things, honor was the driving force behind Abraham's obedience. He sought to honor God with his life, and this is one reason we celebrate Abraham as the father of the faith.

You see, every person is either image driven or honor driven. When you are image driven, you are concerned with how people perceive you. You are driven by how you perceive yourself—based on how the advertisers say you are supposed to look—and pursue an image that you feel will make you happy and accepted by others. At the heart of these concerns are vanity, pride, and ego.

However, as we've studied earlier in the book, God looks at the heart, and He does not care what other people think—or even what you think about yourself. God is unconcerned with image, and in fact, it says God uses the foolish to confound those who think they are wise. I am very sure that God's "foolish" people do not have the image Madison Avenue says they should have.

Honor in the sight of God is a far greater commodity than anything else in life. God is not interested in what kind of house you live in or what kind of car you drive. He's not against good houses or cars. But His interest is how you use those things to bring glory and honor to Him, and so being honor driven should be the ultimate goal of a follower of Jesus Christ.

Every one of us should be putting our hands on the Bible and taking an oath, as we talked about earlier, to live our lives to the honor and glory of God.

Your image will vacillate with time, while honor is timeless. My image of myself is about twenty-one years old—and then I step in front of a mirror. My image has vacillated, dropped, drooped, and fallen off. But the honor of my life is going to be timeless. Your image may change, but honor will follow you into eternity.

Image is driven by appetite and ambition. People who are image-driven have image in the driver's seat. It's a gnawing, nagging driving force based upon appetite and ambition.

Honor, however, is motivated by being conscious of God and aware that your life is an eternal investment. I see honor motivating the young men and women of our armed forces who sign up for the military. Knowing full well it could put them in harm's way, they put the honor of their nation, their families, and their values ahead of their own lives.

If you take a soldier who is image-driven and signed up just to get ahead or because he liked the uniform, I will show you a coward who will buckle when it gets uncomfortable for him to take a stand. However, if you show me a soldier who is honor-driven, I'll show you a true warrior—the kind we should be for God's kingdom.

In the same way, being driven by honor will cause you to say no to lusts. Being driven by honor will cause you to make right choices for right reasons, even if it appears to be to your own detriment. Being honor-driven means when you give your word, whether or not it is in a written contract, you keep it. Being honor-driven means your word is your bond and you do what you say with integrity.

Being honor-driven will cause you to stay in a marriage when everything is old, you've lost common ground, or are mad at one another. Thank God that my wife doesn't need a man with a full head of hair to honor me—she entered into covenant with me, and hair or no hair, she gave her word before God and is sticking with it! It is the same with me for her; I gave my word. And this is God's desire for all of us—that we honor one another and Him especially.

We all yearn for the supernatural-working power of God to flow in our church services and lives. We should all want to see people divinely healed, with blind eyes opened, the lame walking, and deaf ears hearing. We want to hear prophecies and words from the Lord and see other powerful moves of God, but it is no coincidence that people who are not committed to honor and obedience do not experience mighty moves of God.

We pay a "price" to experience God's presence—the price is immediate, unwavering obedience to Him. The price means that we put aside our own desires, our disobedience, our procrastination, and our image-driven lifestyle and choose to establish honor as our moral duty and life compass. We choose obedience over vacillating or disobeying, no matter the real or perceived consequences.

I believe honor is the most important feature of living a Christian life. In fact, every one of the Ten Commandments speaks directly to honor. Obviously, we are directly called to honor our father and mother, but we honor no other gods before Him, do not take the name of the Lord in vain, and remember the Sabbath—and these all honor the Lord. We are called to not murder, commit adultery, steal, or disobey God's other commandments, not just to honor Him but because He desires honor to be such a part of our lives that we would even honor one another.

The Christian life is about *honor*. So what drives you? Honor, or image?

Do You Obey or Flatter?

Some time ago our church purchased a synagogue to use as a new location, and by the first or second meeting we had there, our attendance nearly doubled. I was standing up front and worshiping the Lord, and the presence of God was very strong. I felt like He spoke to me and said, "Sit down." His tone was stern—and as close to hearing an actual voice from heaven as I've ever experienced. The Spirit of God told me to write.

He told me, "Worship and praise, if not followed by obedience, is reduced to a mere attempt to flatter God." Powerful words! Read them again, and let them truly sink in: Worship and praise, if not followed by obedience, is reduced to a mere attempt to flatter God.

> **W**ORSHIP AND PRAISE, IF NOT FOLLOWED BY OBEDIENCE, IS REDUCED TO A MERE ATTEMPT TO FLATTER GOD.

Many people and even entire churches are trying to *flatter* God, because they are not following their praise and worship with *obedience*. People and churches that hear the Word and *obey* are the ones of substance. They are the ones who find that their honor follows them into eternity.

In fact, Jesus puts it bluntly: those who hear God's Word and do it are His family (Luke 8:21). *"And everyone who hears these words of Mine and does not do them will be like a stupid (foolish) man who built his house upon the sand,"* He says in Matthew 7:26 (AMP).

I told you how important it is to ask God to examine your heart repeatedly in this book. It is especially important here: if you are a worshiper and praise the Most High God with your lips on Sunday, you must ensure that you are not living the opposite lifestyle Monday,

Tuesday, Wednesday, and the rest of the week. It is time to ask God to show you what is truly in your heart and whether you are flattering Him or really being one of His disciples by obeying Him.

Fortunately for all of us (for all of us have sinned and fallen short of His glorious standard) God is like a parent interested in instructing us. Let me use the example of a little child in a worship service. Imagine a child turning around and looking at the people around him and smiling and getting attention. That child is not worshiping, and he needs to be taught to focus on Jesus and not to worry about the people around him. The wise parent does not just reprimand the child and tell him to sit down; we must point him in the right direction—toward Jesus. Toward obedience.

The same is true of God, our Father. He seeks to instruct you, to redirect you toward the right way to live the walk of faith. He desires obedience, not sacrifice. He desires that you hear what He has to say—and then do it.

Honor is the Test

God is not looking for flattery—in fact He's looking for the opposite. The Scripture says, "*These people honor me with their lips, but their hearts are far from me*" (Matthew 15:8 NLT). If you want the blessing of God, it must be based on an honor-driven lifestyle—and giving honor to God is the test. Life is God's test—will you honor and obey Him, or will you do your own thing?

Let us come back to Abraham again. God spoke to Him, gave him an assignment, and Abraham passed the test. He honored God above all else—his flesh and blood, his hope for the future, and the very promise God had given to him.

We read in Hebrews it was by faith that Abraham offered Isaac as a sacrifice when God was testing him. Abraham was ready to sacrifice his only son, even though God had told him that Isaac was the son through whom his descendants will be counted. Abraham reasoned that if Isaac died, God was able to bring him back to life again. And in a sense, Abraham did receive his son back from the dead.

Abraham passed God's test, and it showed evidence of his heart to God. And in proving his heart to God with action, God was able to give him the highest honor—founding the nation through which the Savior would come.

I think it is important for us to ask ourselves in brutal honesty, would we do the same? And if we think so, we must ask if we have a track record to back that statement up. Abraham had obeyed God in other things, had failed occasionally, and yet had proved himself obedient to God by honoring Him. He passed the test (Hebrews 11:17-19).

Your life is God's test for you to pass. Will you honor Him?

The Church Must Mature

I was greatly moved by the plight of orphans and lost children their community calls "garbage children" in Brazil. God used one committed Catholic priest, who accepted an assignment from God to help thousands of children the rest of this world has written off. When I met him, he had holes in his shirt, unkempt hair, and a straggly beard. Those who judge by appearance and who are image driven would write him off as surely as the children for whom he cares.

But God is using this man in Brazil, and the Holy Spirit used this priest to convict me that much of what we do in our churches is just flattery to God. He ran up to me, speaking rapidly and passionately in Portuguese, which I do not speak. If I didn't know better, I would have thought he was angry—he was sweating, and the veins were popping in his head.

But he was not angry—he was passionately trying to convey something. "The world is waiting for your church to mature," he told me through an interpreter. It went through me like a sword thrust into my heart. *The rest of the world is waiting for the Church in America to mature.* It's waiting for us to *obey*, and to honor God not just with our lips but also with our actions.

This worn peasant priest, so small to the world's eyes yet so close to the heart of God, got through to me. I teach differently now than before this encounter. Why do I talk of honor, of obedience, of passing the test? Because the rest of the world is waiting for us to use what God has so richly given us to carry out His assignments on the earth. I am desperate to help the Body of Christ mature—to grow up and get our eyes off ourselves and our own concerns and onto a lifestyle of honor and obedience, for these are elements of a mature walk with God. And that is what will leave a legacy.

I find myself wanting to build orphanages at this time of my life. I have seen how God is using the so-called garbage children to instead be children of light, turning their nation to God. I have seen a little girl in Africa whom the Lord raised *from the dead*, literally. Her entire village came to Christ because they saw her funeral procession and then two ordinary African Christian men asked the village chief if they could pray for her. They did—they prayed and asked God to raise her from the dead! They stepped out in obedience, and God moved mightily—not just in the life of that girl and her family, but also in the lives of the people of an entire village.

You will not likely find these men's names on Christian TV, but their names are written in the annals of heaven!

God's test for you may take you around the world or around the corner, but the impact of your obedience, touching just one person, could be profound and resonate in eternity. It is vital to establish a lifestyle of honor and obedience, for we cannot judge between God's small tests and His big ones—we will never know when something seemingly insignificant might change the world and bring honor to Him.

Shallow Repentance Makes for Shallow Christians

We may be tempted to think that repentance for our sins is simply telling God we're sorry and asking for forgiveness. But as I stated earlier, that is not enough—it requires turning from a sinful course and making it right. Obedience is required for *true* repentance. If you just tell God you're sorry, it is a shallow repentance—not really repentance at all. And shallow repentance makes for shallow Christians.

> OBEDIENCE IS REQUIRED FOR TRUE REPENTANCE.

Shallow repentance creates people who will only serve God when it's convenient. But if they're ever asked to lay their life down in a place like Pakistan, India, Eretria, or Sudan for the testimony that Jesus is real in their life, they break under the pressure. But if you are a person who is committed to honoring God with your life, when He calls you to something, you will obey. And if you fail, you will repent, go back, and make it right by doing as He instructed.

Show me honor-driven churches filled with people who obey the Lord, and I will show you people who would no more cheat on their families than slit their own wrists. I will show you people who do what they say they will do, whose word is their bond, and who are faithful to the smallest assignment of God. I will show you people who will smuggle Bibles into China, who will share the gospel in closed Muslim nations, and who will stay true to their testimony when faced with persecution even unto death.

Closer to home, if you show me an honor-driven businessman, I will show you someone who does not just sit back to enjoy a life of ease but who invests his finances for an eternal reward by putting them into the Kingdom of God. Show me an honor-driven husband, and I'll show you a man who is faithful to his wife with his eyes, his affections, and his time. Show me an honor-driven woman, and I'll show you a mother who is patient and shows Christ's love to her squalling, trying children.

Show me honor-driven churchgoers, and I'll show you people like those from my own congregation, going to South America on short-term missions. Every nail they drive, well they dig, and wall they paint is an act of obedient maturity and a chance to practically impact children who can come to know Jesus because ordinary people were honor driven and came to live out the gospel in front of them.

You do not need to be called to preach to reach lives; you only need to honor God with your life and obey. That is your test.

The world is waiting for us to mature. So is God. Will we pass the test? Will we leave a lasting legacy behind, our honor following us into eternity?

21
YOUR LEGACY TO THE NEXT GENERATION

Legacy is the infrastructure of civilization; it is the heritage left behind to our children by the honor with which we live our lives. It is the driving force behind our actions.

Legacy is not generally on the mind of young men, though people like Alexander the Great and others who made massive impacts on the world at an early age may be an example. This is unfortunate, because it shows that for a large portion of our lives, we can be living for only ourselves and not with a view that we are a community of generations.

At this stage in my life, I am examining my legacy—what am I leaving behind to my children and to the lives of the people I have touched? The things of this world are of less importance to me now, and I am thinking of what happens after I am gone. What will I leave behind that will endure?

My children are my biggest legacy, in the same way that I am living out the legacy my father left to me. His righteousness, commitment, and mission mindset have all carried on into my own ministry, and I hope the foundations of honor and responsibility and obedience that I have sought to pass on in my own ministry will continue on in the lives of my physical and spiritual children.

My wife Sharon and I recently moved into a beautiful new home, which you might think would be an ambition of my heart. But instead of feeling that I have somehow attained something, it instead put my mind on how the resource of this home can be used after we are gone. The Lord has been dealing with me to set up a trust in the name of the church and leaving my home to this trust so that when Sharon and I go to heaven, the trust can sell the home and use the proceeds to build an orphanage somewhere in the world.

Leaving an estate is one element, but I seek to leave my children and grandchildren not a legal obligation but a spiritual legacy of outreach. My successors will have a spiritual role in overseeing this legacy and taking care of orphans God loves but who were not born in the United States and our wealth. That legacy will extend to my sons and grandchildren, a spiritual commission to the lost and disadvantaged that must come with the estate I leave to them so that the monies I leave behind are an eternal investment in the prosperity of their very souls.

I seek to leave behind connections to my children as well, relationships that have poured into me. At one point, Marilyn Hickey and Theo Wolmarans nominated me to be on Dr. David Yonggi Cho's board, pastor of the largest church in the world, Yoido Full Gospel Church. My father introduced me to influential men and women of God who have left a spiritual legacy, and I have relished introducing my sons to men like Dr. Cho and the members of his board. This is handing down a spiritual DNA, a spiritual legacy that is even more powerful than the physically inherited characteristics I gave to my children.

We are a civilization of generations, and as a legacy of those who touched my life and influenced my course, I seek to pass generational positives and spiritual DNA on to another generation in turn. I have physical sons who are following my steps, but I also have many spiritual sons and daughters—across the United States and even the world. Spiritual legacy knows no boarders, as evidenced by ministry we are doing in Russia that can trace its legacy back to prayer groups my father hosted.

Your legacy can be incidental, or it can be intentional. God began calling me to think intentionally about it years ago, and it has impacted how I perceive ministry. I pray it has impacted other lives as well, making disciples as Jesus commanded us to do in the Great Commission.

> **Y**OUR LEGACY CAN BE INCIDENTAL, OR IT CAN BE INTENTIONAL.

Our Legacy to the Next Generation

I have a great passion for the next generation because I see where they are headed without the proper biblical culture and the challenges they face from their educational institutions, entertainment, and society at large.

A few years ago, the Southern Baptists put out a report saying that they were losing over *eighty percent* of the kids to secularism when they went to a secular university. They accepted Darwinism, humanistic mindsets, and completely different values. Four out of five of them accepted the corrupted culture of their campus.

This really disturbed me. Southern Baptists have the greatest programs for children—they are arguably the premier Sunday school organization in the world. So if they're losing over eighty percent of their kids, Sunday school must not have done its job, and even our preaching must not have done its job in our pulpits on Sunday.

It says we are failing to leave a legacy to our children. We as a Church are failing to address the subjects of our modern culture in a way that transmits godly values to the next generation. This book is partly my answer to that failure—to make you more intentional about the legacy you leave behind.

This is especially important for pastors, who disciple so many spiritual children as well as physical ones and whom God charges to pass on spiritual DNA. The concept of Sunday school is perhaps three hundred years old, but obviously by itself is not preparing our youth to go out into the world as salt and light.

So if Sunday school is failing us, I believe it is time to turn our lives and our churches into spiritual legacy centers—culturally relevant training centers for the next generation. It is time to get our fight back, to tell our adversary he cannot have our children, and to leave a legacy to your children of godliness.

Legacy is the sum total of all action, qualities of character, spiritual belief, and motives which become an individual's established historical relevance that can be observed and memorialized so as to be passed on to future generations. It is time to combat secularism and the moral decay of our culture in ways that make sense to our children and to give them the backbone and a legacy of obedience that they can in turn give to their children.

You must be intentional in your thinking. You must be intentional about building a legacy, about leaving a tradition of godliness to your children that they embrace. That is what this book is about—a call to intentionally look at your life in light of leaving a legacy that stretches back to Abraham and out into eternity after you are gone.

Jesus said that if we have seen Him, we have seen the Father. If we know Him, we know the Father. He was living out the Father's legacy, and He chose twelve men to pass that on to the next generation. He told them to reach their city, state, country, and then the world—and to in turn pass on that legacy. This was the genesis of apostolic succession we talked about earlier, and God seeks to empower each of you to be an apostle of legacy to your literal and spiritual children.

Every one of us must understand we are living a legacy. We have a responsibility to not only live our lives but to pass on the spiritual legacy we have inherited. I pray that this book has helped bring this to your awareness and to equip you with the tools to live it out.

Now go out and live a life well lived, leaving a legacy of which God can be proud.

ABOUT THE AUTHOR

BISHOP PAUL ZINK is the founding pastor of New Life Christian Fellowship in Jacksonville, Florida, which has been a highly influential inter-denominational church since its inception in 1984. He is also the founder of Providence School, which provides superior college preparatory, Christian education for students from kindergarten through high school. Bishop Zink is an internationally acclaimed conference speaker and is renowned as a pastor, mentor, teacher, and apostolic leader. From 1996 to 2003, Bishop Zink served on the Board of Regents of Oral Roberts University and currently serves on the Board of Directors of Church Growth International in Seoul, Korea, chaired by Dr. David Yonggi Cho. In 2003, he was consecrated as a Bishop in Apostolic Succession through the International Communion of Christian Churches, a ministry committed to restoring the historical unity of the Body of Christ. He has a passion for living life to the fullest of God's calling and leaving a legacy that will influence generations to come.

Bishop Zink and his wife Sharon reside in Jacksonville, Florida and have three married sons and ten grandchildren.

PRAYER

We hope you enjoyed this book and that is has been both a blessing and a challenge to your life and walk with God. Maybe you just got hold of it and are looking through before starting. We made the decision as a publishing company right from the start never to take for granted that everyone has prayed a prayer to receive Jesus as their Lord, so we are including that as the finale to this book. If you have never asked Jesus into your life and would like to do that now, it's so easy. Just pray this simple prayer:

Dear Lord Jesus,
Thank You for dying on the cross for me. I believe that You gave Your life so that I could have life. When You died on the cross, You died as an innocent man who had done nothing wrong. You were paying for my sins and the debt I could never pay. I believe in You, Jesus, and receive the brand new life and fresh start that the Bible promises that I can have. Thank You for my sins forgiven, for the righteousness that comes to me as a gift from You, for hope and love beyond what I have known and the assurance of eternal life that is now mine.
Amen.

Good next moves are to get yourself a Bible that is easy to understand

and begin to read. Maybe start in John so you can discover all about Jesus for yourself. Start to pray – prayer is simply talking to God – and, finally, find a church that's alive and get your life planted in it. These simple ingredients will cause your relationship with God to grow.

Why not email us and let us know if you did that so we can rejoice with you?

info@greatbiglifepublishing.com

ARE YOU AN AUTHOR?

Do you have a word from God on your heart that you're looking to get published to a wider audience?

We're looking for manuscripts that identify with our own vision of bringing life-giving and relevant messages to Body of Christ. Send yours for review towards possible publication to:

Great Big Life Publishing
Empower Centre
83-87 Kingston Road
Portsmouth
Hampshire
PO2 7DX
info@greatbiglifepublishing.com

www.ingramcontent.com/pod-product-compliance
Lightning Source LLC
Chambersburg PA
CBHW070557100426
42744CB00006B/317